Ancient Post-Flood History

Historical Documents that Point to Biblical Creation.

Completely Revised With Nine New Chapters

by
Ken Johnson Th.D.

Ancient Post-Flood History

Ancient Post-Flood History, Revised
by Ken Johnson, Th.D.

Printed in the United States of America

ISBN 1449927939
EAN-13 9781449927936

2

Table of Contents

Preface

The biblical book of Genesis, along with other Jewish histories, give great detail into our past. Those who trust these history texts find it easy to reconstruct ancient history. Those who refuse to even look at them will be ignorant of ancient history.

My critics may call me a euhemerist. I am not. "Euhemerism" is defined as the logic fallacy of "assuming that all myths are connected." I do not believe that all myths are connected. If I believe an ancient document that says *some* myths are connected, I am not a euhemerist, I am a non-biased historian.

I am not insisting every detail in this book is 100% correct; but I believe there are many ancient texts with stories and dates that have some truth to them. If we use the Bible as a basis for these other texts, we will have no problem finding the truth.

My prayer is that this book will inspire readers to investigate ancient history for themselves, thereby stripping away the modern myths of "evolution" and "pre-history."

Visit us at http://www.biblefacts.org and let us know what you thought of this book.

Chapter 1
Source Documents

Second Peter 3:3-7 prophesies that in the days before the return of the Lord Jesus, the world would deliberately forget about the Creation and Noah's Flood, calling both myths. We have seen this happen. Secular society has abandoned this biblical knowledge in favor of Hinduism's myth of evolution. As Paul says:

> "they exchanged the truth of God for a lie, and worshiped and served created things rather than the creator." *Romans 1:25 (NIV)*

Worshiping Creation instead of the Creator works well for those who want to forget God, until they go back far enough to see that our histories include Noah's Flood and references to God's Creation. So what did the evolutionists do? Any history text that referred to the Flood or the Creation less than 10,000 years ago is disregarded as myth. As a result, all the ancient history books have been discarded. They have not been destroyed, just covered up. We now have a new period called "pre-history." There really is no pre-history, only history that they do not want us to know about. Daniel 12:4 says in the last days knowledge would increase, so we must seriously search for it. This should encourage us to look for the ancient texts lost long ago. We find this information today in the Dead Sea Scrolls, the Aramaic Targums, and Midrashim (ancient Jewish texts) like the Jasher scroll.

Genesis
Where do we start to look for these "pre-historical" documents? First we need to define our primary history texts, the ones we will use to judge all others. Our first and

most important text is the book of Genesis. But one has to ask the question: *which* book of Genesis? There is a Hebrew version and a Greek version. The stories in each are the same, but the dates given are vastly different. For example, if we go by the Greek versions, Creation would be dated about 5000 to 5500 BC; but if we go by the Hebrew versions, Creation would be dated about 4000 BC.

To support the Hebrew dating system we have:
- The Masoretic Text (the official Hebrew version used by the Jews today, originally created in the middle ages.)
- The Dead Sea Scrolls (Hebrew copies of the scriptures dating from 300 BC.)

To support the Greek dating system we have:
- The original Septuagint (written about 300 BC and abbreviated LXX. This was used by Jesus, the apostles, and the church fathers.)
- Aquilla's LXX (a Jewish version of the Septuagint dating about AD 126, rewritten to oppose Christianity)
- Symmachus' LXX (an Ebionite or cultic Christian version, rewritten to oppose Christianity.)
- Theodotion's LXX (another Ebionite version, rewritten to oppose Christianity.)

In the third century Origen created what is called the "Hexapla." This was a side-by-side parallel Bible of the Hebrew and the various LXX's. Unfortunately, this was destroyed and we cannot be sure which version of the LXX we currently have.

Today we have two Hebrew versions with identical dates, and four LXX's with different dates. In addition, the church fathers usually quote the LXX, but give dates different from the LXX and the Hebrew sources. We also have Josephus' work which is great for information, but Josephus' dates differ from the Hebrew, LXX, and the church fathers. So how do we decide which set of dates is correct?

Both Joshua 10:13 and 2 Samuel 1:18 instruct us to read the Book of Jasher for additional historical information. Though not inspired, Jasher is highly accurate. This work was originally created about 3000 years ago and has three concurrent timelines running through it. Its dates agree with the Masoretic Text and the Dead Sea Scrolls. The book of Jasher is currently available in both English and Hebrew. To my knowledge, it has never been translated into Greek. So, with both the Greek and Hebrew Bibles pointing to this work, which sides with the original Hebrew version of Genesis, the evidence is overwhelming. We will use the Hebrew version of Genesis as our primary history text. This is the version used in KJV, NIV, and most modern Bibles.

Here is a partial list of recommended books from Scripture:

	Book	Reference
1	Book of the Wars of the Lord	Numbers 21:14
2	Book of Jasher	Joshua 10:13
3	Annals of Jehu	2 Chronicles 20:34
4	Treatise of the book of the Kings	2 Chronicles 24:27
5	Chronicles of Kings	Esther 2:23; 6:1
6	Acts of Solomon	1 Kings 11:41
7	Sayings of the Seers	2 Chronicles 33:19
8	Chronicles of King David	1 Chronicles 27:24
9	Chronicles of Gad the Seer	1 Chronicles 29:29
10	Treatise of the prophet Iddo	2 Chronicles 13:22
11	Prophecy of Ahijah the Shilonite	2 Chronicles 9:29
12	Records of Nathan the Prophet	2 Chronicles 9:29
13	Book of Samuel the Seer	1 Chronicles 29:29

Our secondary sources should be any history works that are recommended by the Bible. Although most of these have been lost to us, some have survived. Remember, these are not inspired, so even though they were perfect *history* texts, they have scribal errors in them now, since they are very old.

Book of Jasher
This book is commonly called the Book of Jasher or the *Sepher HaYashar* in Hebrew. Literally translated, the title means the "Book of the Upright." This is the book mentioned in Joshua 10:13 and 2 Samuel 1:18. Paul records the names of the two magicians in Pharaoh's court: Jannes and Jambres, in 2 Timothy 3:8. This story originally occurs in Jasher 79 where these two names are preserved. The names are not found in the Genesis account. Paul seems well acquainted with the story as given in Jasher. The Book of Jasher has the recommendation of Scripture.

> "And the sun stood still, and the moon stayed, until the people had avenged themselves upon their enemies. **Is not this written in the book of Jasher?** So the sun stood still in the midst of heaven, and hasted not to go down about a whole day."
> *Joshua 10:12-13*

> "And David lamented with this lamentation over Saul and over Jonathan his son: Also he bade them teach the children of Judah the use of the bow: **behold, it is written in the book of Jasher**."
> 2 *Samuel 1:18*

> "Now as Jannes and Jambres withstood Moses, so do these also resist the truth: men of corrupt minds, reprobate concerning the faith. But they shall

proceed no further: for their folly shall be manifest unto all men, as their's also was." *2 Timothy 3:8-9*

Although never added to the canon because it was not an inspired work, the Book of Jasher, nevertheless, was originally a highly accurate history book. Over time, a few scribal errors have developed, but since we have multiple timelines running consecutively through it, it is essentially a self-correcting book.

Any book recommended in the book of Joshua had to exist in Moses' or Joshua's time. Therefore, the Book of Jasher has to be at least 3,000 years old. It is quoted liberally by the first century sage Eliezer. It has existed in handwritten Hebrew for centuries. One of the first Hebrew printings was in Venice in AD 1625. It was not translated into English until AD 1840. It is one of the main texts that the Talmud (AD 200-800) and Seder Olam (AD 169) use for their history.

Mormon Corruption?
It has been noted that the publishing company that produced the first English translation of the book of Jasher was a Mormon publishing company. Mormonism has been classified as a cult by Christians since its inception. Many Christians may be concerned that the text itself may be corrupted deliberately by the cult. Since we have the many copies of Jasher in Hebrew and other languages, and the extensive use by rabbis as early as the first century AD, we can be assured any cultic corruption would have been duly noted by Jewish authorities.

Jasher Forgeries
Several forgeries with the name "Jasher" were written during the Middle Ages. These are clearly fake since they

contradict Scripture and occasionally contradict themselves as well. One such forgery was written by a man named Alcuin, and is still available today.

Seder Olam

Seder Olam means "Order of Eternity" in Hebrew. Put together around 169 AD, the Seder Olam draws heavily from Genesis and Jasher but continues where they leave off. Its history continues past the death of Joshua up to the destruction of the Second Temple.

This work shows the ancient rabbis originally believed Daniel 9 prophesied the King Messiah's coming at approximately AD 30-40 and before the destruction of the Second Temple. The Seder Olam indicates the time of the Persian kings lasted 210 years. This time period agrees with all other histories. Revisionist Rabbi Yose taught the rule of the Persian kings was only twenty-four years! The author of the Seder Olam carefully details how revisionist Rabbi Yose also developed two contradicting theories about Daniel 9 pointing to the destruction of the Second Temple. The Seder clearly shows this to be a deliberate attempt to change the prophecies and calendar date by 167 years because the rabbi rejected the true Messiah.

The Talmud later misquoted the Seder Olam as proof of a twenty-four-year Persian reign and changed the duration of the Persian kings to effectively cut out the coming of Jesus, thereby corrupting their own calendar by at least 167 years.

Other Ancient Works

The Ante-Nicene Fathers by Eerdmans Publishing. This ten-volume set contains the writings from the disciples of the apostles down to AD 325.

The Talmud is the definitive text used by the Jews today, originally written from AD 200 to 800. It

11

contains history and legend but denies that Jesus was the Messiah.

Josephus' Antiquities of the Jews is a first century work held in high esteem by both Christians and Jews.

The Dead Sea Scrolls (DSS) contain many copies of the Scripture dating about 1000 years older than the Hebrew Bible we had at the time. Found in 1948, they contain valuable insights for us today.

Dubious Histories

There are several dubious historical works dating from the Middle Ages. They contain either dates vastly different from Genesis and Jasher, or stories that completely contradict Genesis and Jasher, or in many cases, both. That does not mean that they are totally useless. They may contain some truth, but these should be looked upon with great suspicion. Here is a partial list:

Annius of Viterbo	The Travels of Noah in Europe
Holinshed's Chronicles	

Conclusion

- Our primary source text to study history is the Hebrew version of Genesis.
- Our secondary source is the Book of Jasher
- Our third set of sources are Jewish and Christian historical writers: all the early church fathers, Josephus, Eusebius, Dead Sea Scrolls, Seder Olam, and the Talmud.
- Lastly, secular histories: Egyptian, Tyrian, Babylonian, Greek, and Latin texts. These will be judged by the first three sets of sources.

Gregorian and Jewish Calendars

Our primary source documents will be the book of Genesis and the Jewish history book of Jasher, with commentary from the book of Josephus, so we need to show the difference between the Gregorian and Jewish Calendars.

In America we use the Gregorian calendar, a calendar based on the time when Jesus was born. If our calendar has not been corrupted, the year AD 2010 would mean that Jesus was born 2,010 years ago. Any date before that would be BC. The abbreviation AD stands for "Anno Domini" which is Latin for "in the year of our Lord," meaning the year since our Lord was born. The Jews use a different calendar system based on the creation of the world. So, if you look at a Jewish calendar, you will see that the year AD 2010 is 5770 AM. If the Jewish calendar has not been corrupted, the year 5770 AM would mean that the world was created 5,770 years ago. The abbreviation AM stands for "Anno Moundi," which means "in the year of the world" or, since God created this planet.

When we add all the dates from Adam to Noah's flood from the fifth chapter of Genesis, we conclude the Flood happened 1,656 years after Creation. (See details in chapter two.) On the Jewish calendar, that would be the year 1656 AM. Using the book of Jasher, we learn that the Exodus from Egypt was 2,448 years after Creation or 2448 AM. This leaves a time period of 792 years from Noah's Flood to the Exodus from Egypt under Moses. Since we do not know exactly when the Flood occurred on the BC calendar, we will use the Jewish calendar in this book.

The Flood	792 Years	Exodus
1656		2448

For your general information, the Exodus is thought to have been about 1453 BC and the Flood about 2250 BC. Even with a give or take of 100 years, we can reshape our history into a much more accurate system than the evolutionists do, who try to expand history into thousands and millions of years.

Other important dates on this timeline will be the birth of Abraham in 1948 AM and the fall of the Tower of Babel in 1993 AM.

For an *approximate* BC date, just take the date given in this book and subtract 3925 from it. For Example: the Flood was 1656 AM. Subtract 1,656 from 3,925 and you get 2,269 or 2269 BC.

One Final Note:
There are those who side with the Greek dating system of Creation, beginning at 5500 BC. They reason the Jews deliberately altered the Hebrew text to force the Scripture to point away from Jesus coming as Messiah 2000 years ago, and that the Greek writers kept the correct dating system. As we have seen, there is no Greek version of Jasher or any other secondary version with a different dating system. So there is no reason to assume that the Hebrew text was altered in ancient times.

However, in more recent times the Hebrew text was altered. Scholars have long debated why the Jewish calendar is missing 167 years during the reigns of the Persian kings. The Seder Olam reveals exactly how a rabbi named Yose caused this to occur (see above). The Talmud takes Rabbi Yose's theory and adds to it that Darius the Mead, Cyrus the Persian, and Daruis' son, Xerxes, were all the same person. This misinformation became the first tampering with the timeline.

Until apostasy hit the Jewish nation in the first century, no tampering with the calendar was done. There are enough quotes from very ancient Jewish sources to prove this. So, we do not have to worry about premeditated timeline alterations in the first 3000 years of history.

The following chart compares the dates given in various manuscripts for the time from Creation to the Flood, by showing the age of the father at the birth of his son. Adam was created in the year one and Seth was born when Adam was 130 years old. The chart continues until Noah was 600 years old when the Flood came. The correct set of numbers is in the Hebrew version of Genesis.

Chart of Years (Creation to the Flood)

Name	Hebrew Genesis	Book of Jasher	Greek Genesis	Josephus
Adam	**1**	1	1	1
Seth	**130**	130	230	230
Enos	**105**	105	205	205
Kenan	**90**	90	190	190
Mahalalel	**70**	70	170	170
Jered	**65**	65	165	165
Enoch	**162**	62*	162	162
Methuselah	**62**	62	165	165
Lamech	**187**	187	167	187
Noah	**182**	182	188	182
The Flood	**600**	600	600	600
Total	**1656**	1656	2242	2256

* corrected to 162

Ancient Hebrew Scrolls Hold the Key

Chapter 2
Basic Chronology

This first chart shows the events we use for chronology for the pre-Flood era. The date of the Flood was 1656 AM, or 1,656 years after Creation. The record of the Flood can be found in Genesis 7:11, Jasher 6:1, and in the Seder Olam, chapter 1. The Seder Olam is not broken down into verses.

Event	Bible	Jasher	Seder	Date
Adam created	Gen. 5:1	1:1	1	1
Seth born	Gen. 5:3	2:1	1	130
Enos born	Gen. 5:6	2:2	1	235
Cainan born	Gen. 5:9	2:10	1	325
Mahalalel born	Gen. 5:12	2:15	1	395
Jared born	Gen. 5:15	2:37	1	460
Enoch born	Gen. 5:18	2:37	1	622
Methuselah born	Gen. 5:21	3:1	1	687
Lamech born	Gen. 5:25	3:13	1	874
Noah born	Gen. 5:28,29	4:1	1	1056
Flood occurred	Gen. 7:11	6:1	4	1656

Genesis 11:10 records Shem's son, Arphaxad, was born two years after the Flood. This would have been 1658 AM. From Genesis, Jasher, and the Seder Olam, we find Abraham was born just 292 years after the Flood.

Event	Bible	Jasher	Seder	Date
Arphaxad born	Gen. 11:10	7:19	1	1658
Selah born	Gen. 11:12	7:19	1	1693
Eber born	Gen. 11:14	7:19	1	1723
Peleg born	Gen. 11:16	7:19	1	1757
Reu born	Gen. 11:18	7:22	1	1787
Serug born	Gen. 11:20	7:22	1	1819
Nahor born	Gen. 11:22	7:22	1	1849
Terah born	Gen. 11:24	7:22	1	1878
Abraham born	Gen. 11:26	8:51	1	1948

We can calculate the dates from Abraham's birth all the way to Joshua's death just by using Scripture alone. These other texts simply confirm our calculations.

Event	Bible	Jasher	Seder	Date
Abraham born	Gen.11:26	8:51	1	1948
Abraham given prophecy	Gen. 15:13	13:17	1	2018
Isaac born	Gen. 21:5	21:1	1	2048
Jacob born	Gen. 25:26	26:16	3	2108
Joseph born	Gen. 30:24	31:21	2	2199
Joseph enslaved	Gen. 37:2	41:9	2	2216
Joseph vice-Pharoh	Gen. 41:46	49:38	2	2228
Seven-year Famine began	Gen. 41:54	50:19		2237
Jacob migrated to Egypt	Gen. 47:28	55:26	2	2238
Jacob died	Gen. 47:28	56:1	2	2255
Joseph died	Gen. 50:26	59:25		2309
Kohath	Ex. 6:18		3	2216
Amram	Ex. 6:20		3	
Moses born	Ex. 2:2,10	68:4		2368
Exodus	Ex. 12:41	81:3	3	2448
Moses died	Deut. 31:1-2	87:10	10	2488
Joshua died	Jos. 24:29	90:47	11	2516

The Exodus Date

To calculate the time from the birth of Abraham to the Exodus from Egypt, we need to look at two main Scriptures. In Genesis 15, God gave Abraham a prophecy that after 430 years, God would give his descendants the land of Israel for a homeland. Paul said the 430 years was calculated from the time God gave the prophecy to Abraham to the Exodus from Egypt.

> "The agreement God made with Abraham could not be canceled 430 years later when God gave the law to Moses" *Galatians 3:17 (NLT)*

The book of Exodus shows this prophecy was fulfilled on the *exact day* it was prophesied to be.

> "Now the sojourning of the children of Israel, who dwelt in Egypt, was four hundred and thirty years. And it came to pass at the end of the four hundred and thirty years, even the selfsame day it came to pass, that all the hosts of the LORD went out from the land of Egypt." *Exodus 12:40-41*

Our extra-biblical sources show Abraham was seventy at the time of the prophecy. This fits because another part of the prophecy predicted that his seed would dwell in lands not theirs for four hundred years. Abraham's seed (Isaac) was born when Abraham was one hundred. Isaac's birth was exactly four hundred years before the Exodus from Egypt!

> "And he said unto Abram, Know of a surety that thy seed shall be a stranger in a land that is not theirs, and shall serve them; and they shall afflict them four hundred years;" *Genesis 15:13*

You might ask: what about Exodus 12:40? It clearly says they will "sojourn four hundred years in Egypt!" This is one time that the LXX and the Samaritan Pentateuch really clarify that Scripture. Both add two words to the end of the sentence: literally, "sojourn four hundred years in Egypt *and Canaan.*" Also notice that Exodus 12:41 says this prophecy was fulfilled to the day.

> "And the sojourning of the children of Israel, while they sojourned in the land of Egypt and the land of Canaan, was four hundred and thirty years. And it came to pass after the four hundred and thirty

years, all the forces of the Lord came forth out of the land of Egypt by night." *Exodus 12:40-41 LXX*

You only "sojourn" in a land you do not own. Stephen explained this as well in Acts 7:4-5. They sojourned in Egypt *and Canaan* until the time of Moses when God gave Abraham's offspring, now a nation, the Land of Israel for a possession.

Is there any *other* evidence that the four-hundred-year sojourn was not in Egypt alone?

Genesis 46:27 states that seventy people left Canaan to go to Egypt. In Acts 7:14 we discover that seventy-five people arrived in Egypt. Where did the other five come from? Five babies were born along the way to Egypt. One of these was Jochebed, daughter of Levi and mother of Moses. (Jasher 59:9)

Also notice in Genesis 46:11 that Kohath, son of Levi, was among those who went to Egypt with his grandfather, Jacob. Kohath was the grandfather of Moses.

Jasher dates Israel's migration to Egypt to the year 2238 AM and the Exodus at 2448 AM.

These dates divide the four hundred and thirty years as follows: the sojourn in Egypt two hundred and ten years, and the time spent in Canaan, two hundred and twenty years. This equals the four hundred and thirty years found in Galatians 3:17.

Event	Bible	Jasher	Seder	Date
Abraham born	Gen. 11:26	8:51	1	1948
Abraham's Prophecy	Gen. 15:13	13:17	1	2018
Isaac born	Gen. 21:5	21:1	1	2048
Exodus	Ex. 12:41	81:3	3	2448
Temple Dedication	1 King 6:1,38		15	2935
Shishak's Invasion	2 Chr. 12:2		16	2969
Temple Destruction			28	3338

Exodus to Solomon's Temple

In 1 Kings 6, verses one and 38 we are told there were 480 years from the Exodus to the start of the building of Solomon's Temple. We also find that it took seven years to finish building the temple. Solomon's Temple was dedicated 487 years after the Exodus, or in the year 2935 AM. This was 2,935 years after Creation.

> "And it came to pass in the four hundred and eightieth year after the children of Israel were come out of the land of Egypt, in the fourth year of Solomon's reign over Israel, in the month Zif, which is the second month, that he began to build the house of the LORD." *1 Kings 6:1*

> "And in the eleventh year, in the month Bul, which is the eighth month, was the house finished throughout all the parts thereof, and according to all the fashion of it. So was he seven years in building it." *1 Kings 6:38*

Destruction of Solomon's Temple

Depending on how we calculate the events recorded in the books of Kings and Chronicles, we may come up with the time Solomon's Temple stood, ranging from 380 years to 410 years. The Seder Olam, Talmud and other sources state the time period was exactly 403 years. This places the destruction of Solomon's Temple by the Babylonians in 3338 AM, or 3,338 years after Creation.

Date of Creation

We have shown from Jasher that from Creation to the Exodus is 2,448 years. We are told in 1 Kings 6:1 that from the time of the Exodus to Solomon's laying the foundation stone of the temple in the fourth year of his reign, was 480 years. This would put the start of the building at 2928 AM. It took seven years to finish, according to 1 Kings 6:38, which was Solomon's 11th year.

This agrees perfectly with both the Seder Olam and Talmud which have the Exodus in 2448 AM, the laying of the foundation stone in 2928 AM, and the dedication of the temple in 2935 AM.

The Seder Olam's history continues after Jasher ends and stops at the destruction of the second temple. The Talmud's history continues even further. Since we know about the discrepancy in the Persian era, we can't use the Seder Olam or Talmud from the Persian period forward. The most reliable place to stop using them is with the destruction of the first temple.

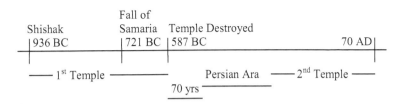

We need to look at three dates to come to a conclusion. Secular history records the Assyrians captured Israel (Samaria) in 721 BC. The Babylonians destroyed the first

Temple in 587 BC, and Pharaoh Shishak invaded Judah between 921 BC and 936 BC.

The difference between 721 BC and 587 BC is 134 years. The Seder Olam and the Talmud give the dates of 3205 AM for the fall of northern kingdom of Israel and 3338 AM for the fall of Jerusalem and the destruction of the first Temple, a difference of only 133 years. This is only a one year difference from secular history. The invasion of Shishak is given at 2969 AM.

If we conclude that the dates for the fall of Samaria and the destruction of the first Temple are more accurate than the invasion of Shishak, then 3,338 years added to 587 BC would put the year of creation at 3925 BC. If we believe the invasion of Shishak, ranging from 923 BC to 936 BC, to be more accurate, then 2969 added to these dates would place Creation between 3892 BC and 3905 BC.

I believe that we should take the fall of Samaria and the destruction of the first Temple for our calculation because they are closest to our time and the most attested to. That would place creation at 3925 BC, the Flood at 2269 BC, the Exodus at 1477 BC.

3/1477   —   3925 BC ①   2269 BC ②

This is why some scholars place the Flood at approximately 2250 BC and the Exodus at approximately 1450 BC, but we will use the Jewish calendar for all the dates in the rest of this book.

3925 BC   Creation
2269 BC   Flood
1477 BC   Exodus

Codex Judaica

Modern Orthodox Jews still use the ancient Jewish Calendar. Mattis Kantor created the Jewish Timeline Encyclopedia in AD 1994. It was re-released in AD 2005 as the Codex Judaica. It is

Codex Judaica	
Creation	1 AM
The Flood	1656 AM
Abraham's birth	1948 AM
The Exodus	2448 AM
Temple dedication	2935 AM
Temple destruction	3338 AM

hard to know exactly where these dates occur on the AD/BC timeline but all the basic dates of the Codex Judaica agree with those of the Bible, Jasher, and Seder Olam.

Possible Dates for Creation

Many Christian and Jewish historians have worked with these books and created their own timetables. As you can see from the chart at the right when they use the Hebrew manuscripts their calculations are very close.

Historian	Creation
Eusebius	3942 BC
Jerome	3942 BC
Venerable Bede	3944 BC
James Usser	4004 BC
Joseph Scaliger	3949 BC
Isaac Newton	3940 BC
Mattis Kantor	3760 BC
Robert Killian	3892 BC
Ken Johnson	3925 BC

The Pre-Flood History That Started It All

Chapter 3
Pre-Flood History

The Bible tells us all life on earth was completely destroyed by a flood of water. Only Noah, his wife, their three sons, and their wives, with the animals, escaped on the ark to repopulate the planet.

Adam and Eve waited for God's promise of a redeemer. They had many children. Their third son was named Seth. He was born in the year 130 AM.

Adam's Prediction
Adam prophesied that the world would be destroyed once by fire and once by a flood of water; but he was not sure which would occur first. He taught these prophecies to his children, along with his first-hand experience of the Fall of Man and God's promise of a redeemer.

> "upon Adam's prediction that the world was to be destroyed at one time by the force of fire, and at another time by the violence and quantity of water, they made two pillars, the one of brick, the other of stone: they inscribed their discoveries on them both, that in case the pillar of brick should be destroyed by the flood, the pillar of stone might remain, and exhibit those discoveries to mankind; and also inform them that there was another pillar of brick erected by them. Now this remains in the land of Siriad to this day." *Josephus 1.2.3*

First Apostasy
When Seth was 105 years old, he fathered a child he named Enos. Enos was born in the year 235 AM. The book

of Jasher states that at this time the first wave of apostasy began.

"And Seth lived one hundred and five years, and he begat a son; and Seth called the name of his son Enosh, saying, Because in that time the sons of men began to multiply, and to afflict their souls and hearts by transgressing and rebelling against God. And it was in the days of Enosh that the sons of men continued to rebel and transgress against God, to increase the anger of the Lord against the sons of men." *Jasher 2:2-3*

"And the sons of men went and they served other gods, and they forgot the Lord who had created them in the earth: and in those days the sons of men made images of brass and iron, wood and stone, and they bowed down and served them. And every man made his god and they bowed down to them, and the sons of men forsook the Lord all the days of Enosh and his children;" *Jasher 2:4-5*

In reaction to this idolatry, God caused a flood to occur that destroyed a large amount of crops; and, afterwards, God caused a draught to occur. This did not lead to repentance on the part of the idolaters. For a complete detail on the pre-flood pagan religion, see the book *Ancient Paganism* by the author.

"And the Lord caused the waters of the river Gihon to overwhelm them, and he destroyed and consumed them, and he destroyed the third part of the earth, and notwithstanding this, the sons of men did not turn from their evil ways, and their hands were yet extended to do evil in the sight of the Lord. And in those days there was neither sowing nor

27

reaping in the earth; and there was no food for the sons of men and the famine was very great in those days." *Jasher 2:6-7*

First Revival

When Enos was ninety years old, he fathered a child he named Cainan. Cainan was wise and walked in the way of his great-grandfather Adam. Adam instructed Cainan about the Fall, the promised redemption, and the world's destruction by water and fire.

Cainan was wise enough to understand that since God sent a warning flood and famine because of idolatry, that the part of Adam's prophecy of a worldwide destruction by water would occur before the world's destruction by fire.

"And Cainan knew by his wisdom that God would destroy the sons of men for having sinned upon earth, and that the Lord would in the latter days bring upon them the waters of the flood. And in those days Cainan wrote upon tablets of stone, what was to take place in time to come, and he put them in his treasures." *Jasher 2:12-13*

Cainan began to preach repentance. After a few people began to repent and be converted, Adam decided that if he made Cainan reign as king in his place, Cainan might be able to start the revival Adam could not. So when Cainan was forty years old, in the year 365 AM, Adam made Cainan king. Cainan was successful in leading a small revival.

"And Cainan reigned over the whole earth, and he turned some of the sons of men to the service of God." *Jasher 2:14*

Second Apostasy

This revival lasted little more than forty years. Jasher records that during the lifetime of Cainan's son Mahalalleel, somewhere between 395 and 460 AM, the revival ceased and men began to rebel once again. This time the apostasy involved more people than before. Someone during this time invented an herb potion that caused miscarriages. From that time forward abortions were common place, and this angered God considerably.

> "For in those days the sons of men began to trespass against God, and to transgress the commandments which he had commanded to Adam, to be fruitful and multiply in the earth. And some of the sons of men caused their wives to drink a draught that would render them barren, in order that they might retain their figures and whereby their beautiful appearance might not fade." *Jasher 2:19-20*

The apostasy worsened as time went along. But in the year 622 AM, Enoch, the grandson of Mahalalleel, was born. When Enoch was 165 years old, he fathered a child he named Methuselah. After Methuselah was born, Enoch began to grow closer to God and the teachings of our forefather Adam. In time, he began to convert a few people to follow the ways of God.

Second Revival

This was noticed by Cainan who was still ruling at the time. Cainan believed Enoch was anointed by God in a very special way. Cainan chose to relinquish his throne and make Enoch king, in the year 687 AM.

Enoch led the most powerful revival in the history of the pre-flood world. This revival lasted longer than any other.

The 700's AM were marked with many turning to the service of the Lord. But this began to wane in the 800's AM.

Worship of Saints
A very strange thing began to occur among the believers. People who truly were worshipers of God fell into a trap set by Lucifer and the fallen angels.

These believers were influenced by the manners and customs of the pagans around them, and unknowingly began to adopt their ideas and mannerisms. They began to honor godly *people* more highly than they should. This created a type of idol within the true religion that abhors idols. Religious books and other objects became nothing more to them in time than holy relics. These things were simply misused.

As much as Enoch tried to counter this behavior, it was to no avail. More and more frequently, Enoch witnessed religious people venerating relics. He began to see a kind of worship directed to him rather than to God. As a result, Enoch withdrew from public life.

He sequestered himself in his mountain home. His days were filled with the worship of God. He spent less and less time with people. This did not help the situation, either. When retiring did not work, he came back to his public life to teach and sternly warn them; but his warnings never really took hold.

So with Enoch's presence causing more harm than good, the Lord told Enoch that he would be taken away. Enoch then warned his son to try everything he could following his Rapture to turn the people's focus back to God and God alone.

Great Apostasy

In the year 987 AM, Enoch made his son Methuselah king and prepared to be Raptured. After Enoch's Rapture, Methuselah held control over the kingdom but his power waned quickly. Around the year 1000 AM, men began to rebel again and the Lord sent another famine. They ignored the warning and wickedness continued until every man had an idol in his own house. They began to use science to anger God (Jasher 1-5).

> "And their judges and rulers went to the daughters of men and took their wives by force from their husbands according to their choice, and the sons of men in those days took from the cattle of the earth, the beasts of the field and the fowls of the air, and taught the mixture of animals of one species with the other, in order therewith to provoke the Lord; and God saw the whole earth and it was corrupt, for all flesh had corrupted its ways upon earth, all men and all animals." *Jasher 4:18*

Since God is angered at cross breeding His creation, we are probably angering Him with our present day genetic experiments and attempts at cloning. What did Jesus say?

> "But as the days of Noah were, so shall also the coming of the Son of man be." *Matthew 24:37*

The Cainites

While this was going on, a great war was brewing. The Hebrew historian, Josephus, wrote about the history of the Sethite-Cainite Wars. Josephus revealed to us:

Adam's son Cain traveled far away from the land of Eden and founded a city, naming it after his firstborn son. In the course of time the descendants of Adam had spread out over the earth. There were several nations between the land of Nod and the land occupied by some of the descendants of Seth. Slowly the Cainite ways were adopted by all except the Sethites. Up until the Rapture of Enoch, the seventh generation from Adam, the Sethites lived in peace.

> "Now this posterity of Seth continued to esteem God as the Lord of the universe, and to have an entire regard to virtue, for seven generations; but in process of time they were perverted, and forsook the practices of their forefathers; and did neither pay those honors to God which were appointed them, nor had they any concern to do justice towards men. But for what degree of zeal they had formerly shown for virtue, they now showed by their actions a double degree of wickedness, whereby they made God to be their enemy." *Josephus 2.3.1*

How did this occur? When Enoch was no longer ruling on earth, the Cainites made their move. Josephus says Cain:

> "became a great leader of men into wicked courses. He also introduced a change in that way of simplicity wherein men lived before; and was the author of measures and weights. And whereas they lived innocently and generously while they knew nothing of such arts, he changed the world into cunning craftiness. He first of all set boundaries about lands: he built a city, and fortified it with walls, and he compelled his family to come

together to it; and called that city Enoch, after the name of his eldest son Enoch…" *Josephus 1.2.2*

One of Cain's descendants was Tubal. Tubal was the first martial artist. The rabbis state he invented the perfect murder weapon, the sword. He followed in the ways of Cain.

> "But Tubal, one of his children by the other wife, exceeded all men in strength, and was very expert and famous in martial performances. He procured what tended to the pleasures of the body by that method; and first of all invented the art of making brass." *Josephus 1.2.2*

The Cainites waged war with the now complaisant Sethites, who thought they were following God, but were more obsessed with orders and relics.

> "Nay, even while Adam was alive, it came to pass that the posterity of Cain became exceeding wicked, every one successively dying, one after another, more wicked than the former. They were intolerable in war, and vehement in robberies; and if anyone were slow to murder people, yet was he bold in his profligate behavior, in acting unjustly, and doing injuries for gain." *Josephus 1.2.2*

Another trick of Satan is to get your eyes off God. Instead of trusting Him as your avenger, you seek your own justice, becoming very similar to those you seek to eliminate.

Homosexual Marriage
There has always been homosexuality. It has always been classified as a sin before God. The Canaanites practiced homosexual rituals in the worship of their gods and

goddesses, but since the time of Noah there has never been a nation that sanctioned homosexual marriage. But the rabbis state this did occur right before Noah's Flood. This may have been a part of the pre-flood religion; or it just may have been a result of it. See *Ancient Paganism* for a full discussion of the pre-flood pagan religion.

In Romans 1, the apostle Paul seems to indicate that idolatry produced immorality; and together idolatry and immorality caused the Great Apostasy. That, in turn, resulted in extreme forms of homosexuality, which caused God to destroy the world.

> "Professing themselves to be wise, they became fools, And changed the glory of the uncorruptible God into an image made like to corruptible man, and to birds, and fourfooted beasts, and creeping things. Wherefore God also gave them up to uncleanness through the lusts of their own hearts, to dishonour their own bodies between themselves: Who changed the truth of God into a lie, and worshipped and served the creature more than the Creator, who is blessed for ever. Amen. For this cause God gave them up unto vile affections: for even their women did change the natural use into that which is against nature: And likewise also the men, leaving the natural use of the woman, burned in their lust one toward another; men with men working that which is unseemly, and receiving in themselves that recompence of their error which was meet. And even as they did not like to retain God in their knowledge, God gave them over to a reprobate mind, to do those things which are not convenient." *Romans 1:22-28*

The ancient rabbis seem to believe this also. They stated the practice of ordaining homosexual marriage was the last step in the downward spiral that caused God's judgment.

"Rabbi Huna said in the name of Rabbi Joseph, 'The generation of the Flood was not wiped out until they wrote marriage documents for the union of a man to a male or to an animal.'" *Genesis Rabbah 26:4-5; Leviticus Rabbah 23:9*

"Rabbi Hiyyah taught: The passage reads 'I am the Lord, your God' two times – I am the One Who punished the generation of the Flood, and the people of Sodom and Gomorrah, and Egypt; and in the future I will punish those who do as they did. The generations of the Flood were kings, and were wiped off the earth when they were soaked in sexual sin." *Leviticus Rabbah 23:9 (commentary on Leviticus 18:3)*

"And what did they do? A man got married to a man, and a woman to a woman, a man married a woman and her daughter, and a woman was married to two (men). Therefore it is said, "And you shall not walk in their statutes" *Sifra Acharei Mot, Parashah 9:8 (Commentary on Leviticus 18:3)*

The Flood

At this point the whole world grew totally apostate. Only Noah and his immediate family stood firm in their zeal for God.

"But Noah was very uneasy at what they did; and being displeased at their conduct, persuaded them to change their dispositions and their acts for the

> better: but seeing they did not yield to him, but were slaves to their wicked pleasures, he was afraid they would kill him, together with his wife and children, and those they had married; so he departed out of that land." *Josephus 2.3.1*

In 1536 AM God commanded Noah to preach repentance with the warning that if mankind did not repent within 120 years, God would destroy the earth with a Flood. Noah and Methuselah preached for 120 years without a single convert. Then, on the seventeenth day of the second month in the year 1656 AM, God destroyed the world by the Flood (Genesis 7, Jasher 6). This was exactly one week after Methuselah died peacefully in his sleep.

> "In the six hundredth year of Noah's life, in the second month, on the seventeenth day of the month, on the same day all the fountains of the great deep burst open, and the floodgates of the sky were opened." *Genesis 7:11 NASB*

> "In the second month, on the twenty-seventh day of the month, the earth was dry." *Genesis 8:14 NASB*

One year and ten days later, Noah and his family went out from the ark into a new world. This was the 27th day of the second month, in the year 1657 AM.

Pre-Flood Patriarchs
The following is a chart of the ten pre-flood patriarchs and their names as found in ancient records around the world. This will cover the first 1,656 years. The Hebrew names are from Genesis; the Hindu names are from the Hindu poems Vaivasvata, Satyavarman, and Matsya Purana. The Babylonian names came from Berosus, the Chaldean, and

the Sumerian names are derived from the Weld-Blundell Prism (WB-62) King List. Chinese names are compiled from Chinese legend and the oral traditions of the Miao people.

Hebrew	Babylonian	Hindu	Sumerian	China
Adam	Alorus		Alulim	Fu Hsi
Seth	Alaparus		Alalgar	Shen Nung
Enos	Amelon		Kidunnu	Yen Ti
Cainan	Ammenon		Alimma	Huang Ti
Mahalaleel	Megalarus		Enmenluanna	Shao Hao
Jared	Daonus		Dumuzi	Chaun Hsu (Kao Yang)
Enoch	Euedoreschus		Ensipazianna	K'u
Methuselah	Amempsinus		Enmendurann	Yao
Lamech	Otiartes		Sukurlam	Shun
Noah	Xisurthrus	Satyavarata	Ziusudra	Yu

Josephus wrote that Berosus recorded an extremely accurate and very detailed account of history starting from Adam through the Flood and continuing with the Chaldean kings. Very little has survived from Berosus' history books.

> "Now all the writers of barbarian histories make mention of this flood, and of this ark; among whom is Berosus the Chaldean. For when he is describing the circumstances of the flood, he goes on thus: 'It is said there is still some part of this ship in Armenia, at the mountain of the Cordyaeans; and that some people carry off pieces of the bitumen, which they take away, and use chiefly as amulets for the averting of mischiefs.'"
> *Josephus 1.3.6*

Josephus continued writing that many of the ancient historians recorded the Flood and the chronologies. Still existent in his time were: Hieronymus the Egyptian who

37

wrote the Phoenician Antiquities, Mnaseas, Manetho who wrote the Egyptian History, Mochus, Hestieus, Hesiod, Hecatseus, Hellanicus, Acusilaus, Ephorus, and Nicolaus.

> "Nicolaus of Damascus, in his ninety-sixth book, hath a particular relation about them; where he speaks thus: 'There is a great mountain in Armenia, over Minyas, called Baris, upon which it is reported that many who fled at the time of the Deluge were saved; and that one who was carried in an ark came on shore upon the top of it; and that the remains of the timber were a great while preserved. This might be the man about whom Moses the legislator of the Jews wrote.'" *Josephus 1.3.6*

There are over 600 different flood legends from around the world. Even though they differ in details, their very existence proves there really was a world-wide flood.

The Garden of Eden
Many have asked the question, "where was the Garden of Eden located?" If we compare the ancient history texts, we can come to a conclusion.

> "And a river went out of Eden to water the garden; and from thence it was parted, and became into four heads. The name of the first is Pison: that is it which compasseth the whole land of Havilah, where there is gold; And the gold of that land is good: there is bdellium and the onyx stone. And the name of the second river is Gihon: the same is it that compasseth the whole land of Ethiopia. And the name of the third river is Hiddekel: that is it which goeth toward the east of Assyria. And the fourth river is Euphrates." *Genesis 2:10-14*

Genesis 2:10-14 shows the location of the Garden of Eden was where four rivers met. For each land and river mentioned in Genesis, Josephus (Antiquities 1:3) gives their Greek names and meanings.

Name	Meaning	Land
Pison (Ganges)	Multitude	Havilah (India)
Gihon (Nile)	That which raises from the east	Cush (Ethiopia and/or Egypt)
Diglath (Tigris)	Swift and Narrow	East Ashur (Iraq)
Phrath (Euphrates)	Dispersion or a Flower	Iraq

If this is correct, the Nile at one time flowed from the east. Before a major continental shift occurred, the Ganges and Nile would have to have flowed differently to meet the Tigris and Euphrates.

Genesis states the Tigris bordered the Land of Ashur or Assyria. So this has to be the current Tigris and Euphrates in the land of Iraq.

When we look closely at the Table of Nations, we see two close descendants of Noah had the name "Havilah." One is the son of Cush, whom the Greeks call the Getuli, and the other is the son of Joctan, son of Eber, who settled in the area of the Copan River in India and beyond.

The Targum of Genesis 2:11 identifies India as Havilah. Josephus, like the Targum, assumes the land of Havilah is the one settled by the sons of Joctan.

If Josephus is mistaken and Havilah is the Cushite tribe, then the Phison is in the area of Saudi Arabia, probably the Wadi Batan. If so, the Gihon would be the Karun River which "arises from the east" and empties into the Persian Gulf.

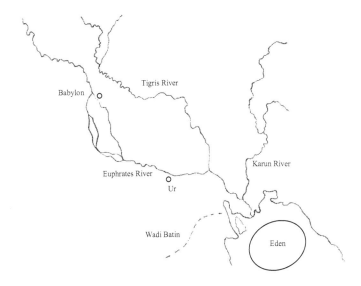

Josephus says the river encircled the earth. The Hebrew word for earth is Eretz. It can also be translated land. If the land of Eden was an island at the tip of the Persian Gulf, the Persian Gulf itself would look like a river encircling the "land" of Eden. Water from the four rivers would meet to water the island and also empty into the gulf.

In any case, the location of Eden has to be where the Tigris and Euphrates empty into the Persian Gulf.

Questions:
There are several common questions raised when reading the first ten chapters of Genesis. Here are the answers to those questions from our ancient source documents:

1. How many Children did Adam and Eve actually have?

    a. Multiple records state besides children specifically named, they had "many other children."

2. When did Cain kill Abel?

    a. The *Jewish Timeline Encyclopedia* places this in the year 41 AM, citing rabbinical tradition.

3. Where did Cain get his wife?

    a. Cain married his sister, as did all first generation people. (Josephus Ant 1:2). The *Book of Jubilees* tells us her name was Awan.

4. Where is the Land of Nod?

    a. No credible records exist identifying the exact location, but Genesis 2 places it somewhere on the east side of Eden. (See the paragraph on Eden.)

5. Were the seven days of creation really 24-hour days or a longer length of time?

    a. Josephus says they were 24-hour days, because Genesis uses the phrase "evening and morning" (Josephus Ant 1:1)

6. Did it really take 120 years to build the Ark?

    a. No. Genesis six shows man was given 120 years to repent. When man did not respond, God commanded the Ark be built. It actually took five years to build the Ark (Jasher 5:34)

7. Who was Noah's wife?

    a. The prophetess Naamah, the daughter of Enoch. This would make her Noah's great aunt. Noah was 498 and she was 580 when they married. (Jasher 5)

8. Who were the wives of Shem, Ham, and Japheth?

    a. They were the three daughters of Eliakim, son of Methuselah. (Jasher 5) This would make Shem's wife his first cousin once removed. Not much is recorded about them, but there are legends.

9. I always hear the phrase, "Shem, Ham, and Japheth." Does that mean Shem was the oldest?

   a. No. Noah was 500 when he started having children. Shem is the most important to the Jews so he is usually listed first.

   b. Japheth was born in 1556 AM when Noah was 500 and Naamah was 582. Shem was born in 1558 AM when Noah was 502 and Naamah was 584. We have no record of Ham's birth. (Jasher 5)

   c. This is why Genesis 11:10 says Shem was 100 at Arphaxad's birth, two years after the Flood.

After the Flood...

Chapter 4
The Immortals

Shem		600
Arphaxed, Selah, Eber		438
Peleg	239	

In the chart above, the lines show three different sets of lifespans ranging from the 600's to the 400's and 200's.

We know that Shem lived to the age of 600, which was 500 years after the flood. The first three generations born after the flood lived 400 plus years. The fourth generation and the generations afterwards (Peleg and his descendants.) lived only a little more than 200 years.

> "...to Eber were born two children, the name of one was Peleg, for in his days the sons of men were divided, and in the latter days, the earth was divided. And the name of the second was Yoktan, meaning that in his day the lives of the sons of men were diminished and lessened." *Jasher 7:19-20*

What happened to decrease the lifespan after the Flood from the 400-year range to the 200-year range?

Most creation scientists believe the pre-deluvian world was covered by a canopy of water vapor. (Genesis 1:6-9, Josephus called this a crystalline firmament – Ant 1:1) The firmament protected the earth by blocking out most of the cosmic radiation and increasing the atmospheric pressure. When the Flood caused the collapse of the water canopy, less pressure and more radiation cut mankind's lifespan to less than half of what it was before the canopy dissolved.

Some suggest a residue of the canopy formed an ice ring, similar to the ice rings around Saturn. This ice ring may have helped block out some cosmic radiation. At about the time of Peleg, the ice ring collapsed, which allowed more radiation to bombard the planet and cut human lifespan in half yet again. (See "The World that Perished" Video.)

Genesis and Jasher identify the dramatic lifespan change after the Flood, the secondary change at Peleg's time, and the gradual drop off of each generation's age after that.

Shem died at 600	Peleg died at 239	Abraham died at 175
Arphaxad died at 438	Reu died at 239	Isaac died at 180
Selah died at 433	Serug died at 205	Jacob died at 147
Eber died at 464	Nahor I died at 148	Joseph died at 110
	Terah died at 205	Moses died at 120

Regardless of what caused the second change to the human lifespan, let's assume that Shem, Ham, and Japheth (and their wives), all born before the flood, would live to be around 600 years old. All their children born before the collapse of the ice ring would live about 425 years. Everyone born after the rings' collapse would only live to about 200 years.

If this is true, then we can see how several myths might develop. First, people who only live to about 200 years old would consider those living much longer to be immortals, and *their* parents, who apparently will never die, to be gods. But, when the first three generations start dying off, rumors will develop about wars between the immortals and gods. After the languages change at the Tower of Babel, the legends would have been even more confused with a variety of different names applied to each "immortal" or "god." We will see how this develops into the various religions in the following chapters.

The Apostasy

What started false religions? In the beginning everyone knew Noah and believed in the one true God. The Scriptures call Babylon the mother of all false religions, because under Nimrod the original false religious system was successfully implemented. We learn from the church fathers that the root of this madness started with the sons of Ham.

> "Fallen angels taught men the use of magical incantations that would force demons to obey man. After the flood Ham the son of Noah unhappily discovered this and taught it to his sons. This became ingrained into the Egyptians, Persians, and Babylonians. Ham died shortly after the fall of the Tower of Babel. Nimrod, called Ninus by the Greeks, was handed this knowledge and by it caused men to go away from the worship of God and go into diverse and erratic superstitions and they began to be governed by the signs in the stars and motions of the planets."
>
> *Recognitions of Clement 4.26-29*

Nimrod turned the government into a tyranny and set up twelve idols of wood named after the twelve months of the year, each representing a sign of the Zodiac. He commanded everyone to worship each idol in its proper month. (Jasher 9:8-10)

If everyone believed in the one true God, how did the sons of Ham convince people otherwise? You can't just invent stories about other gods out there. No one will believe you.

Pantheism

The first thing they did was teach that the one true Creator God is merely a completely impersonal force. They also started teaching that all of creation is a part of the original God. This is called pantheism. They added that everything else father Noah taught was correct.

At a certain point, many in the apostasy started calling themselves "immortals," and their parents, "gods." They created temples for themselves. They explained "a god is simply one blessed by the one true God and allowed to rule, a godly man." The temples they built were no more than embassies for the visiting ruler, built out of respect to the ruler and God, or so they were told.

Later the concept of immortals and gods became common. The people who objected to this teaching were then told the one true God does exist; but, when He created the gods, He put a little of Himself into them. So the new gods are an incarnation or manifestation of the original God.

When that lie became commonplace, they changed the teaching to say that the one true Creator God *emptied* Himself into His highest creations, "the gods" and *ceased to exist*. Eventually the true God was forgotten or replaced by the little gods.

Later, ancestor worship was added and new gods formed. At this point we see three major forms of false religion.

Hinduism, Wicca, and the Sons of Ham

Hinduism breaks off at the point where God is impersonal but still exists. Their form of polytheism is the worship of a little god that represents an aspect of the one true God (like war, love, sex, etc.)

Wicca breaks off at the point of saying the original creative force, whatever it was, emptied itself into creation and thus is no more. People are now the highest form of life/god.

The sons of Ham originally taught that with the one God/force emptying Himself into just certain people, this created a few little gods to be worshiped by man. There is no emanation of the original God in mankind.

All of these religions include a reference to the one true God. They worship idols under slightly different theologies and astrology. See chapter on Ancient India for more details.

The Seven Noahide Laws

We are first introduced to the Noahide laws in the Talmud, written between AD 200 and AD 800. In Genesis 9:1-7 God commanded Noah to instruct all his children to institute capital punishment in their governments. They are allowed to eat meat, but must first drain the blood from it. Eating blood is prohibited.

The Talmud (Sanhedrin 56a) states that Noah commanded his children to set up governments to establish nations. He commanded every nation to observe seven laws. They may add laws to the seven, but never override the original seven. Later, under Moses, God commanded the nation of Israel to observe Ten Commandments; but these were not designed for Gentile nations. This is why most Christians worship on the Lord's Day, Sunday, instead of observing the Jewish Sabbath, on Saturday.

The Seven Noahide Laws

1. **Do not worship idols**
   Worship the one true God alone.
2. **Do not commit blasphemy**
   Cursing the name of God is forbidden. We must honor and respect God in our speech.
3. **Do not murder**
   The death penalty is for murderers, administered if there is one testifying eyewitness.
4. **Do not commit sexual sins**
   Incest, adultery, bestiality, homosexuality, and rape are forbidden.
5. **Do not steal**
6. **Do not eat blood or flesh cut from a living animal**
   This also includes the ethical treatment of animals.
7. **Establish courts of justice**
   Create courts to enforce the first six laws and create new useful laws or customs.

Taken from the Talmud; Sanhedrin 56a.

Some Jewish converts thought that all Christians must observe the laws of Moses (like the Sabbath) and the laws instituted under father Abraham (like circumcision). The Jerusalem council decided these kinds of laws were not binding on Christians. They concluded:

> "For it seemed good to the Holy Spirit and to us to lay no greater burden on you than these requirements: You must abstain from eating food offered to idols, from consuming blood or eating the meat of strangled animals, and from sexual immorality. If you do this, you will do well."
> *Acts 15:28-29 NLT*

In other words, only the laws instituted by father Noah (like not eating blood), are binding on all mankind, since we are all his children.

Ancient Post-Flood History

On March 20, 1990, President George Bush signed into law a historic Joint Resolution of both Houses of Congress recognizing the Seven Noahide Laws as the "bedrock of society from the dawn of civilization" and urged our country to "return the world to the moral and ethical values contained in the Seven Noahide Laws" (H.J. Res. 104, Public Law 102-14). ·

Church Fathers Clement of Alexandria (ECF 2.77) and Tatian (ECF 2.143) tell us that the ancient Romans and barbarians considered homosexuality and pederasty crimes punishable by death. In the first century, however, homosexuality and pederasty were widely practiced by the Romans.

In the following chapters we will see how each Gentile nation was set up and the problems encountered by not following father Noah's commands.

Information taken from church fathers Lactantius *Divine Institutes*, Tertullian *Gods of the Heathen*, and Arnobius *Against the Heathen*.

Post-Flood Histories

Chapter 5
Europe, Africa, and Asia

⊢◁⟙×⟙⟙⟙𝌆⟙⟙⟙⟙⟙⟙⟙⟙⟙⟙⟙⟙⟙⟙⟙⟙⟙⟙⟙⟙⟙⟙⟙
Linear B Hieroglyphics

/60 to 1200 years after Flood

About one hundred to two hundred years after the Flood, Noah gave the lands that we call Europe and Asia to his son Japheth; Africa to his son Ham; and the Middle East extending to India to his son Shem. Each of the three sons divided their portion among their children.

Japheth / Europe

The description of Japheth's area is very clear. His land included all of Europe from Spain to Scandinavia. It included Russia, with Kazakhstan, Uzbekistan, Kyrgyzstan, Tadzhikistan, and Mongolia. It also included the top half of the Caspian Sea, along with Georgia, Armenia, and Turkey.

> "Japhet, the son of Noah, had seven sons: they inhabited so, that, beginning at the mountains Taurus and Amanus, they proceeded along Asia, as far as the river Tansis, and along Europe to Cadiz; and settling themselves on the lands which they light upon, which none had inhabited before, they called the nations by their own names."
> *Josephus Ant.1.6.1*

> "And for Japheth came forth the third portion beyond the river Tina to the north of the outflow of its waters, and it extends north-easterly to the whole region of Gog, and to all the country east thereof. And it extends northerly to the north, and it extends to the mountains of Qelt towards the

north, and towards the sea of Ma'uk, and it goes forth to the east of Gadir as far as the region of the waters of the sea. And it extends until it approaches the west of Fara and it returns towards 'Aferag, and it extends easterly to the waters of the sea of Me'at. And it extends to the region of the river Tina in a north-easterly direction until it approaches the boundary of its waters towards the mountain Rafa, and it turns round towards the north. This is the land which came forth for Japheth and his sons as the portion of his inheritance which he should possess for himself and his sons, for their generations for ever; five great islands, and a great land in the north. But it is cold, and the land of Ham is hot, and the land of Shem is neither hot nor cold, but it is of blended cold and heat." *Jubilees 9:24-30*

Japhetic Rivers, Mountain Ranges, and Cities

Tina River	Oxis River - Amu Darya
Tanis River	Don River in Russia
Abysses	?
Me'at Sea	Artic and North Atlantic Oceans
Ma'uk Sea	Baltic Sea
Egyptian Sea	Red Sea
Gihon River	Ganges River
Great Sea	Mediterranean Sea
Rafa Mts.	Himalayan & Pamir Mountains
Tarus Mts	Southern Turkey – Euphrates flows from Tarus Mts
Amanus Mts.	Nur Mountains in S. Turkey
Libabus Mts.	Lebanon
Celtic Mts.	Pyrenees?
Karaso	?
Cadiz/Gadir	Cadiz Spain
Fara	?
'Aferag	Africa
Five Islands	Balearic, Sicily, Sardinia, Crete, & Cypress

The Me'at Sea is the great sea that encircled the earth. It included the Arctic, North Atlantic and Indian oceans. The Mediterranean Sea may have been thought to be a part of it, since it is connected to the Atlantic.

Gadir is the ancient name of Cadiz, Spain, the oldest continually occupied city in Europe.

The Celtic Mountains would be one or more of the mountain ranges in the lands of the Celts, namely Germany and/or France.

Shem / Middle East

The land of Shem extended from the Mediterranean Sea to the east including Lebanon, Syria, Iraq, Iran, Turkmenistan, Afghanistan, Pakistan, India, and the Arabian Peninsula. The Arabian Peninsula included the United Arab Emirates, Oman, Yemen, Saudi-Arabia, Jordan, Sinai Peninsula, Gaza, and Israel.

"...from the middle of the mountain range of Rafa, from the mouth of the water from the river Tina, and his portion goes towards the west through the midst of this river, and it extends till it reaches the water of the Abysses, out of which this river goes forth and pours its waters into the sea Me'at, and this river flows into the great sea. And all that is towards the north is Japheth's, and all that is towards the south belongs to Shem. And it extends till it reaches Karaso: this is in the bosom of the tongue which looks towards the south. And his portion extends along the great sea, and it extends in a straight line till it reaches the west of the tongue which looks towards the south: for this sea is named the tongue of the Egyptian Sea. And it turns from here towards the south towards the mouth of the great sea on the shore of (its) waters, and it extends to the west to 'Afra, and it extends till it reaches the waters of Arabia and Ophra, and to the south of the waters of Gihon, to the banks of this river. And it extends towards the east, till it reaches the Garden of Eden, to the south thereof, [to the south] and from the east of the whole land of Eden and of the whole east, it turns to the east and proceeds till it reaches the east of the mountain named Rafa, and it descends to the bank of the mouth of the river Tina. This portion came forth by lot for Shem and his sons…" *Jubilees 8:12-17*

"Shem, the third son of Noah, had five sons, who inhabited the land that began at Euphrates, and reached to the Indian Ocean." *Josephus Ant.1.6.4*

Jubilees described the whole land of Shem. Josephus described the portion of land that remained Shem's after the Hamatic invasion by Nimrod where the Canaanites and other Hamites took control of the land from the Mediterranean to the Euphrates.

Semitic Rivers, Mountain Ranges, and Cities

Tina River	Oxus River - Amu Darya
Abysses	?
Me'at Sea	The sea that circles the earth
Egyptian Sea	Red Sea
Gihon River	Ganges River
Great Sea	Mediterranean Sea
Rafa Mts.	Himalayan & Pamir Mountains
Libabus Mts.	Lebanon
Karaso	?
'Aferag	Africa

Apparently a series of rivers and lakes, called the Abysses, flowed from the Caspian Sea north of Persia and south of Turkey until it reached the Mediterranean Sea.

The Oxis River now flows into the Aral Sea; but it historically flowed into the Caspian Sea.

Ham / Africa

Ham's land is described as the continent of Africa. But it is noted that the descendants of Ham invaded and occupied the territory of Shem from the Mediterranean Sea to the Euphrates River.

> "The children of Ham possessed the land from Syria and Amanus, and the mountains of Libanus; seizing upon all that was on its sea-coasts, and as far as the ocean, and keeping it as their own. Some indeed of its names are utterly vanished away; others of them being changed, and another sound given them, are hardly to be discovered; yet a few there are which have kept their denominations entire. For of the four sons of Ham, time has not at all hurt the name of Chus; for the Ethiopians, over whom he reigned, are even at this day, both by themselves and by all men in Asia, called Chusites. The memory also of the Mesraites is preserved in their name; for all we who inhabit this country [of Judea] called Egypt Mestre, and the Egyptians Mestreans. Phut also was the founder of Libya, and called the inhabitants Phutites, from himself: there is also a river in the country of Moors which bears that name; whence it is that we may see the greatest part of the Grecian historiographers mention that river and the adjoining country by the apellation of Phut: but the name it has now has

been by change given it from one of the sons of Mesraim, who was called Lybyos. We will inform you presently what has been the occasion why it has been called Africa also... Amathus inhabited in Amathine, which is even now called Amathe by the inhabitants, although the Macedonians named it Epiphania, from one of his posterity: Arudeus possessed the island Aradus: Arucas possessed Arce, which is in Libanus. But for the seven others, [Eueus,] Chetteus, Jebuseus, Amorreus, Gergesus, Eudeus, Sineus, Samareus, we have nothing in the sacred books but their names, for the Hebrews overthrew their cities; and their calamities came upon them on the occasion following."
Josephus Ant.1.6.2

Hamatic Rivers, Mountain Ranges, and Cities

Libabus Mts.	Lebanon
Acre	Haifa Bay, Israel
Aradus	Arvad, Tripoli Syria
Amathe	Hama, Syria
Put	Libya
Egyptian Sea	Red Sea
Gihon River	Ganges River
Great Sea	Mediterranean Sea
Tarus Mts	Southern Turkey – Euphrates flows from Tarus Mts
Amanus Mts.	Nur Mountains in S. Turkey
Cadiz/Gadir	Cadiz Spain
Five Islands	Balearic, Sicily, Sardinia, Crete, & Cypress

Table of Nations

Using Genesis, Jasher, and Josephus, we have compiled the following table of nations.

Shem's Sons

Elam	Elamites, Presians
Ashur	Assyrians
Arphaxad	Chaldeans, Babylonains
Lud	Ludites, Lydians
Aram	Aramites, Syrians
Uz	Trachonitus, Damascus
Gether	Bactrians
Mash	Mesaneans, Charax Spasini

Japheth's Sons

Gomer	French, Germans
Ashkenez	Rheginians
Riphath	Bartonim, Ripheans, Paphlagonians
Togarmah	Phrygians, Armenia
Magog	Magogim, Sythians
Madai	Medes
Javan	Greeks, Ionians, Macedonians
Elishah	Aeolians, Lumbardi
Tarshish	Cilicia, Britian
Kittim	Romans
Dodanim	Trojans
Tubal	Iberes, Tuscany, Italy
Sabinah	East Italy
Meshech	Shebashni, Cappadocians, Mongolia
Tiras	Rushash, Thracians, Cushni, Ongolis, Mongolia

Ham's Sons

Cush	Ethiopia
Sheba	Sabaens
Havilah	Getuli
Sabatah	Sabthens, Astaborans
Raamah	Sheba, Dedan, Saudi Arabia
Sabtecha	Sabactens
Mizraim	Egypt
Phut	Lybia

Canaan	Canaanites
Zidon	Sidon city
Arodi	Aradus Island and Arce in Lebanon
Amori	Amoties, Epiphania
Heth *	
Gergashi *	Gergasites
Hivi *	Hivites
Arkee *	Arkities
Seni *	
Zimodi *	
Chamothi *	
Hur**	Seirites

*Destroyed by the Israelites
**Destroyed by the descendants of Esau

Japheth's Descendants

Anglo-Saxons
Armenia
Britain
Denmark & Norway
France & Germany
Georgia
Greece
Ireland
Italy
Russia
Troy

Chapter 6
Anglo-Saxons / England

ABCDEFGHIJKLMNOPQRSTUVWXYZ
Anglo-Saxon Alphabet

The Anglo-Saxons trace their linage from Noah through Japheth (Seskef) down to Odin as the Danish and Norwegians do. Odin was the twentieth generation from Noah. In the chapter on Denmark and Norway, we will combine six ancient manuscripts, thereby recreating a complete list of the twenty generations.

The Anglo-Saxons have their own chronicle, called the Anglo-Saxon Chronicle. There are several copies; but the oldest dates back to AD 547. Today the most complete and commonly read Anglo-Saxon chronicle is called the Parker Chronicle. Historian Nennius gives the same basic linage, but differs in several points of detail. It should be noted that this proves they are not copies of each other, but independent histories with variant spellings of the same names of people.

The following chart is adapted from the Parker Chronicle, which dates from the tenth century. This manuscript is missing the tenth and fourteenth entries. These missing entries will be seen in the chapter on Denmark and Norway.

The Parker Chronicle presents the genealogies of the six royal houses of Kent, East Anglia, Lindsey, Mercia, Northumbri, and Wessex. The manuscript begins with the same list as the Danish and Norwegian king lists, tracing lineages form Noah to Odin. It continues from Odin's children in the twenty-first generation down to the formation of the royal houses.

1. Noe (Noah)
2. Sceaf (Japheth)
3. Bedwig
4. Hwala
5. Hrathra
6. Itermon
7. Heremod
8. Scealdwea
9. Beaw
10.
11. Taetwa
12. Geata
13. Godwulf
14.
15. Finn
16. Frithuwulf
17. Freawine
18. Frealaf
19. Frithuwald
20. Woden

21 Baeldaeg	Winta	Witta	Wihlaeg	Waegdaeg	Caser
22 Brand	Cretta	Wihtgils	Waermud	Sigegar	Tyman
23 Freothogar	Cwedgils	Hengist	Offa	Swebdaeg	Trygil
24 Freawine	Caedbed	Oisc	Angeltheow	Sigegeat	Hrothmund
25 Wig	Bubba	Irminic	Eomaer	Saebald	Hryp
26 Gewis	Beda	Ethelbert	Icel	Saefugel	Wilhelm
27 Esla	Beoscep	Eadbald	Cnebba	Westerfalca	Wehh
28 Elesa	Eanferth	Earconbert	Cynewald	Wilgils	Wuffa
29 Cerdic	Eata	Egbert	Creoda	Uxfrea	Tyla
30 Cynric	Aldfirth	Wictred	Pybba	Yffe	Redwlad
31 Ceawlin	**Lindsey**	Etherbert	Eawa	Elfric	Earpwald
32 Cuthwine		**Kent**	Osmod	**Northumbria**	**E. Anglia**
33 Cutha			Eanwulf		
34 Ceowald			Thincferth		
35 Cenred			Offa		
36 Ingild			**Mercia**		
37 Eoppa					
38 Eafa					
39 Eaalhmund					
40 Ecoryht					
41 Aethelwulf					
42 Alfred the Great					
Wessex					

Alfred the Great founded the House of Wessex. Aldfirth founded the House of Lindsey and Etherbert founded the House of Kent. Offa founded the House of Mercia, Elfric founded the House of Northunbria, and Earpwald founded the House of East Anglia. These six houses form the royalty of the Anglo-Saxons.

Notice the twelfth generation is Geat (Geata). In the epic legend of Beowulf, Beowulf is a descendant of Geat, and came to help the king of Denmark. Whether the legend of Beowulf has a basis in historical fact or not, the lineages of Beowulf, as well as the Danish kings, are accurate.

In time the rulers of the Anglo-Saxons replaced the ruling Britons. The name of the island was changed from Britain to Angle-land, meaning the land of the Angles or Anglo-Saxons. Today the island is called England.

See the chapter on Britain for the history of that people.

Chapter 7
Armenia

Ո Բ Գ Դ Ե Զ Է Ը Թ Ժ Ի Լ Խ Ծ Կ Հ Ձ Ղ Ճ ա բ գ դ ե զ է թ
Armenian Alphabet

The Bible records <u>Togarmah</u> as being the <u>son of Gomer</u>, who was the son of Japheth, who in turn was the son of Noah.

"Now these *are* the generations of the sons of Noah, Shem, Ham, and Japheth: and unto them were sons born after the flood. The sons of <u>Japheth; Gomer,</u> and Magog, and Madai, and Javan, and Tubal, and Meshech, and Tiras. And the sons of Gomer; Ashkenaz, and Riphath, and Togarmah." *Genesis 10:1-3 KJV*

One of the earliest written histories of the Armenian people is dated to the <u>fifth century</u> AD. The *History of Armenia*, written by Moses Chorene, tells the story of how one of the sons of Togarmah founded the Armenian people.

Togarmah had eight sons. Their names are recorded in *History of Armenia 1:1*; and the *Georgian Chronicle 1:1*. The firstborn son of Togarmah, called Hayk by the Armenian people, lived in the area today known as Babylon. Hayk is said to have had seven sons: Armaneak, Aramais, Gegham, Harma, Aram, Ara, and Keghetzig.

Sons of Togarmah
Hayk
Kartlos
Bardos
Movkans
Leks
Herans
Kovkas
Egers

The Armenian people claim Hayk as their founder; but take the name of their country from Hayk's firstborn son Armaneak. Even today near the Armenian capital, there still stands a statue of Hayk, son of Togarmah and founder of the Armenian people.

Hayk, the founder of Armenia.

The *History of Armenia* continues explaining that after the birth of Hayk's firstborn son, Armaneak, Nimrod took control of the known world and formed the first post-Flood empire. While in service to Nimrod, Hayk saw the government became more and more corrupt. Hayk decided to take his family and leave for a place far away from the land of that evil empire.

Hayk, with over 300 of his household, settled in one place and founded a village that he named Hayashen. Today Haykashen is a city in the Armavir Province of Armenia. As of 2008 AD, its population was 1,238.

Hayk also created smaller settlements around the capital city. One outpost that existed on the route back to Nimrod's empire was governed by Hayk's grandson, Kadmos. One of the sons of Nimrod was dispatched to entreat Hayk to return to Nimrod's service and his empire, but Hayk refused.

Nimrod's son returned with a small army of sixty warriors to capture the rebels and bring them back by force. Hayk was warned by his grandson, Kadmos, of the army's approach. He assembled his own army on the shore of Lake Van and commanded them to defeat the invading army and kill the commander, or die trying, rather than become enslaved.

Hayk set a trap in the mountain pass near Julamerk, southeast of Lake Van. In the famous battle of Dyutsaznamart, the invading army was lead by that same son of Nimrod. Hayk fired the first arrow upon their approach, striking and killing Nimrod's son. The army then in disarray was attacked by the Armenians and destroyed. This battle would have taken place sometime between 1950 and 1900 BC.

Later, the Castle of Haykaberd was established on the site of that great battle. Hayk ordered the corpse of Nimrod's son embalmed and buried in a high place in the view of his wives and sons.

Hayk founded the first Armenian dynasty, called the Haykazuni dynasty. The Armenian princely houses, the Khorkhoruni, Bznuni, Syuni, Vahevuni, Manavazian, and Arran trace their genealogy back to Hayk.

Chapter 8
Britain

ABCDEFGHIJKLMNOPQRSTUVWXYZ
British Alphabet

British history is well documented in the writings of Nennius and Geoffrey of Monmouth.

The following list is compiled from their histories. Starting with Noah and extending through the destruction of Troy, it continues with Brutis leading his people to the island of Britain. The British rule continued until the Anglo-Saxons conquered Britain and formed England. For a detailed look at Aeneas and Troy, see the chapter on *Troy*.

1. Noah
2. Japheth
3. Javan
4. Elisha
5. Dardanus *Built city of Troy*
6. Trois
7.
8. Anchises
9. Aeneas
10. Ascanius
11. Silvius
12. Brutis

From the history of Nennius we learn that Dardanus was the son of Elisha, son of Javan, son of Japheth, son of Noah.

Dardanus, Noah's great-great-grandson, built the city of Troy, naming it after his firstborn son, Trois. That means the Trojans are partly Greek by descent.

The great-great-grandson of Trois was the famous Trojan warrior Aeneas (called Angeas by Jasher). We know from Scripture and other Jewish histories that Noah's Flood occurred in 1656 AM. Jasher records Aeneas' death at 2411 AM, 37 years prior to the Exodus from Egypt.

Brutus
The Greeks enslaved the Trojans captured in battle. By the twelfth generation, the great-grandson of Aeneas, Brutis, led a rebellion that freed the descendants of the Trojans.

Brutus lead his brethren though the Mediterranean Sea, past Spain and north to an island then called Albion. Taking the island for themselves, they created a country and called it Britain, based on the name of the founder, Brutus. Later when the Anglo-Saxons invaded, the name of the island was changed to England, which is a shortened version of Angle-land. Brutus and his countrymen created a capital city they called New Troy. Today New Troy is called London, England. New Troy was finished about the time Eli the Priest was ruler in Israel, and the Ark of the Covenant had been captured by the Philistines.

Geoffrey of Monmouth adds a curious note in his history. After New Troy was built, a partly submerged temple dedicated to the false Greek gods Apollo and Minerva was found. It had been there for quite some time and no one ever figured out who built it.

After studying the writings found in the ancient temple, King Baldud ordered the temple to be made usable and he reinstituted necromancy and Minerva worship. Eventually King Baldud was killed while practicing one of those pagan rites. This happened about the time King Solomon of Israel finished building the first Jewish Temple.

The Book of Jasher adds a comment to the early days of Rome. In 2500 AM, Latinus II became king of Rome. In his days he conquered Brittania and Kernania, and the Greeks (children of Elisha, son of Javan). Brittania was an old name for Britain and Kernania was a providence around the area of France, populated by Greeks.

The ancient Hebrew name for the island called Albion, then Britain, and now England, was Tarshish. We can learn about its future by studying the Biblical prophecies about Tarshish.

Chapter 9
Denmark and Norway

Yᛜ ᛁᚠᛚᛏ ᛊᛤᚢᚲᛩ ᛏᛗᛚ<ᛊ ᛁᛜᚷᛖ ᛥᚲᛒᚠ
Danish Runes

Six ancient manuscripts still preserve the linage of the Scandinavian people of Denmark, Sweden, Norway, Iceland, and the Anglo-Saxons.

The Life of King Alfred
  Written in AD 893 by Welsh monk, John Asser.

Cotton MS. Tiberius A,
  An eleventh century Anglo-Saxon chronicle housed in the British museum.

Vetustissima Regum Septentrionis Series Langfethgatal dicta
  A twelfth century Danish manuscript.

Fabii Ethelwerdi Chronicle
  Written by Anglo-Saxon historian, Ethelward.

Corpus Poeticum Boreale
  Written about the twelfth century by Icelandic Historian Prose Edda.

Historia Brittonum
  Written in AD 833 by Nennius.

These six histories show a combined list of twenty generations from Noah to Odin. Scholars have long noted that the Scandinavians refer to Japheth, Noah's son, as

Sceaf. Now if we could identify Bedwig with one of the Hebrew names for Japheth's children, we could move that much closer to mapping out the migrations.

The twentieth generation is Oden or Woden. Oden was the principle ancestor worshiped as a god by the pagan Scandinavians.

Asser	ASC	Lang.	Ethelwerdi	Edda	Nennius
1 Noe	Noe	Noa			
2 Seth	Sceaf	Seskef	Scef	Seskel	
3 Beduulg	Bedwig	Bedvig		Bethvig	
4 Huala	Hwala				
5 Hathra	Hrathra	Athra		Athra	
6 Itermod	Itermon	Itermann		Itrmann	
7 Heremod	Heremod	Heremotr		Heremoth	
8 Sceldwea	Scealdwea	Scealdna	Scyld	Skjaldun	
9 Beauu	Beaw	Beaf	Beo	Bjar	
10					
11 Taetuua	Taetwa		Tetuua		
12 Geata	Geata	Eat	Geat	Jat	Geta
13 Godwulf	Godwulf	Godulf	Godtuulfe	Gutholfr	
14					Fodepaid
15 Finn	Finn	Finn	Fin	Finn	Finn
16 Frithuwulf	Frithuwulf		Frithouulf		Fredulf
17	Freawine				
18 Frealaf	Frealaf	Frealaf	Frealaf	Frinallaf	Frealaf
19 Frithowald	Frithuwald		Frithouuald		
20 Uuoden	Woden	Voden	Uuothen	Othin	Woden

In this chapter we want to look at the Danish and Norwegian chronicles. Each traces their linage from Oden to the start of the royal houses of Denmark and Norway.

The Danish list is the shortest, tracing five generations from Oden to Ingialdr Starkadar and the start of the Royal house of Denmark. The current Royal house of Denmark traces it start back to king Gorm the Old who became the Danish king in 899 AD.

Danish list
Woden
Skjoldr
Fridleirfr
Fridefrode
Frode Fraekni
Ingialdr Starkadar

In other lists we have the approximate date of Ingialdr Starkadar ascending the Danish throne in AD 440.

The ancient Norwegian list is similar to the Danish list. It shows ten generations from Oden to Haralldr Harfagri.

Haralldr Harfagri ascended the Norwegian throne in approximately AD 560.

Norwegian list
Woden
Niodr i Notunum
Yngvifraeyr
Jorundr
Aun
Egill Tunnadolgr
Ottarr Vendilkraka
Athils at Uppsaulum
Eysteinn
Yngvarr
Haralldr Harfagri

Beowulf

Only one manuscript of the epic poem Beowulf still exists. It dates from about AD 1000. Whether or not Grendel and the other flying monsters in the poem are completely imaginary, or based on some now-extinct reptiles, the story has its basis in historical fact.

Beowulf was born in AD 495. He was the son of Ecgtheow. In the year 502, when he was seven years old, he was brought to his grandfather Hrethel for training. Hrethel, king of the Geats, ruled from AD 445 to AD 503.

The Geats were a tribe who inhabited an area in southern Sweden. The founder of the Geats was Geat, the twelfth generation from Noah, according to the Scandinavian king lists (see above). In time they became absorbed by the other peoples around them.

In AD 510, Beowulf fought in the battle of Ravenswood. This was one of many wars between the Geats and other Swedish tribes. Afterwards, when he was twenty years old, he traveled to Denmark and received an audience with Hrothgar, king of the Danes. This was the year AD 515 and where the poem Beowulf begins.

Six years after Beowulf killed Grendel, Beowulf's uncle, King Hygelac, was slain. Hygelac lived from AD 475 to AD 521. He ascended the throne of the Geats in AD 503. King Hygelac is also mentioned in Gregory of Tour's *Historiae Francorum*.

When King Hygelac died, his son Prince Heardred, took the throne and was tutored by Beowulf until he reached the age of maturity. King Heardred lived from AD 511 to AD 533. Upon his death, Beowulf took the throne and ruled the Geats in peace for over fifty years until his death in AD 583. Beowulf was approximately eighty-eight years old at his death.

All of this simply tells us there are numerous historical records we can use to create a consistent history of all nations back to Noah.

Chapter 10
France and Germany

ABCDEFGHIJKLMNOPQRSTUVWXYZ
French and German Alphabet

The French are descended from some of the sons of Gomer.

> "And the children of Gomer, according to their cities, were the Francum, who dwell in the land of Franza, by the river Franza, by the river Senah."
> *Jasher 10:8*

Notice the river "Senah" is virtually the same as the modern spelling of the Seine River, on which Paris, the capital city of France, was built.

> "For Gomer founded those whom the Greeks now call Galatians, [Galls,] but were then called Gomerites." *Josephus Ant. 1.6.1*

> "And the sons of Gomer; Ashkenaz, and Riphath, and Togarmah. *Genesis 10:3 KJV*

Some Irish traditions say Riphath is the ancestor of the Celts and that the Druids originally came from the area of France. Diodorus Siculus and Strabo both stated the Celtic heartland was in southern France and the Gauls were to the north of the Celts. Even so, the Romans referred to both as Gauls.

Josephus wrote that the descendants of Riphath were the the Paphlagonians. Pliny calls Riphath, Riphaci, and mentions a group of mountains named after him, the

Riphæan range. The ancient Greeks and Romans recognized a Riphæan mountain range in the Ural Mountains in Russia and one in Scandinavia. This indicates that their ancestors began in the area of the black sea before they spread to Europe. The Scandinavian Range is also referred to as the Celtic mountains.

> "And the children of Rephath are the Bartonim, who dwell in the land of Bartonia by the river Ledah, which empties its waters in the great sea Gihon, that is, oceanus." *Jasher 10:9*

Josephus states the Greek name for the descendants of Ashkenaz was Rheginians. Ancient Roman maps show the land of the Rheginians to be the same as the modern nations of Poland, Czechoslovakia and Germany to the banks of the Danube River.

> "And the sons of Gomer; Ashkenaz, and Riphath, and Togarmah." *Genesis 10:3 KJV*

The modern Hebrew word for Germany is "Ashkenaz" and German Jews are referred to as Ashkenazic Jews. The Talmud also refers to Ashkenazim as German Jews.

Bartonia	Brittany, France
Ledah River	Lorie River
Gihon Sea	Atlantic Ocean
Senah River	Seine River
Ashkenaz	Germany
Riphæan range	Scandinavia, & Ural Mountains

Chapter 11
Georgia

ა ბ გ დ ე ვ ზ თ ი კ ლ მ ნ ო პ ჟ რ ს ტ უ ქ ღ შ წ ჯ ჭ
Georgian Alphabet

In the chapter on Armenia we learned Togarmah had eight sons. His firstborn founded the Armenian race.

This information was preserved in the *History of Armenia*, by Moses Chorene, and the *Georgian Chronicles* written by Leonti Mroveli in the 11th century AD.

The sons of Togarmah became the progenitors of several of the Caucasian peoples. Togarmah is said to have settled among his children in Armenia and Georgia. It is also said he lived for almost 600 years.

Sons of Togarmah
Hayk
Kartlos
Bardos
Movkans
Leks
Herans
Kovkas
Egers

After the fall of the tower of Babel, when Nimrod lost most of his power in the outer regions, Togarmah partitioned his land among his eight sons. Hayk took what is now Armenia and part of Turkey. Kartlos and his sons settled the regions which today are collectively called the provinces of Georgia. His other sons took the land between the Caspian Sea and the Black Sea up to the Caucasus Mountains. Two of Togarmah's sons, Kovkas and Kekan (founder of the Leks), settled north of the Caucasus Mountains.

The *Georgian Chronicles* tell us the second-born son of Togarmah, Kartlos, founded the Georgian race.

Kartlos had five sons: Mc'xet'a, Gardbos, Kaxos, Kuxos, and Gajis. Mc'xet'a had three sons: Op'los, Ojrxos, and Jawaxos. These seven sons and grandsons of Kartlos became the founders and first kings of the Mtskheta, Gardabani, Kakheti, Kukheti, Gachiani, Uplistsikhe, Odzrkhe, and Javakheti peoples, respectively.

Sons of Kartlos
Mc'xet'a
Gardbos
Kaxos
Kuxos
Gajis

Kartlos united his people and founded the city of Kartli. Today Kartli is the name of the largest province of Eastern Georgia. The Georgian capital, Tbilisi, and the cities Gori and Rustavi are located there. Azerbaijan and Armenia are directly south of it.

Sons of Mc'xet'a
Op'los
Ojrxos
Jawaxos

After the death of Kartlos' son Mc'xet'a, the people fell into disarray, not wanting Mc'xet'a's son Op'los to rule over them. The people rebelled and worshiped the sun, moon, and seven stars. They swore oaths at the tomb of Kartlos.

After some time the Scythian kingdom (Southern Russia) extended further south to the Caucasus Mountains. The Scythians attacked and enslaved the Leks and the Kovkas.

After "much time had passed" the Elamite Empire (Persia, modern Iran) invaded under King Ap'ridon (Faridun of Persian tradition) and took control of Armenia and Georgia from the Scythians.

After Ap'ridon was killed in battle, a new Persian king arose named K'ekapos (Kay Kavus of Persian tradition). A few years after K'ekapos forced Georgia to start paying a yearly tribute, a report spread among all the nations that:

> "Moses, the friend of the great God, had brought the 12 tribes of Israel across the Red Sea, 60,000 strong, and that they were in the desert and eating manna-bread that came down from heaven."
> *Armenian Chronicles 16*

All the heathen nations were astonished upon hearing this. The text continues describing various wars between the sons of Togarmah and the Persians until Alexander the Great conquered the Persian Empire, Armenia, and Georgia.

By the time of Alexander the Great, the Georgians spoke five languages: Armenian, Greek, Hebrew, Syrian, and Scythian. These languages, combined together, became the modern Georgian language.

Alexander discovered the religion of the Georgians had degraded to the worst state he had ever seen. For in the pagan Georgian religion, people married or fornicated with anyone they chose – including family members. They ate everything – including living animals and the corpses of animals and people. The other things Alexander witnessed were too horrific to put down in words. Alexander vowed to extinguish their evil religion.

Part of the house of Togarmah, known as Kipchaks, spread throughout, and intermingled with, the peoples of southern Russia as far as China and as far west as Bulgaria, and the Ukraine. Azerbaijan should be a part of the house of Togarmah; but they have no record that they are.

King Pharnavaz I (299-234 BC) is credited with creating the modern Georgian alphabet. He was the first king of the line of Kartlos to rule over all the Georgians. King Pharnavaz also created an idol of himself, which he placed in the ancient capital of Kartli. All Georgians were commanded to offer sacrifices to it. From the time of Alexander, who abolished this kind of paganism, the Georgians did not eat human beings, but at that time Pharnavaz revived the ancient pagan religion, with its cannibalism, along with his idol, and commanded that human sacrifices to his idol be eaten ritually once again.

Three hundred years later, during the first year of the reign of King Aderki, Jesus Christ was born in Bethlehem, Judea. The Jews living in Georgia heard of the visit of the Persian Magi and thought the Persians were capturing Jerusalem. Upon learning the Persians were giving gifts to the new-born king and Jerusalem was safe, all the Georgian Jews rejoiced.

About thirty years later, it was heard that the Virgin-born child had grown up and was called the Son of God. The Georgian Jews sent two scholars of their law to investigate the matter. They returned with a good report. Sometime thereafter Andrew and Simon the Canaanite came preaching the gospel. The region of the Egris converted to Christianity. This angered King Adrik, who sent his troops in. Simon was martyred in the city of Nikop'is on the Greek border. Andrew escaped without harm; but the region of Egris was forced to reconvert to the native religion.

It wasn't until the fourth century, under the missionary Nino, that Christianity came back to Georgia. Georgia officially became a Christian nation by decree of King Mirian III in the year 337 AD.

From the time of Kartlos, Georgia was called the kingdom of Kartli. The Greeks called it Iberia. The Kartli region and the six neighboring regions were united into one kingdom named Georgia with Tbilisi as its capital in the year AD 1122.

This picture is from the 1700 Vakhtangiseuli edition of the Georgian Chronicles. The drawing is of Togarmos and his sons. Given in order are: Movakans, Bardos, Kartlos, Hayk, Thargamos, Leks, Kovkas, Herans, and Egers.

Chapter 12
Greece

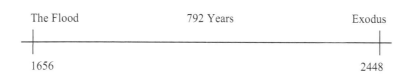
α β χ δ ε φ γ η ι φ κ λ μ ν ο π θ ρ σ τ υ ϖ ω ξ ψ ζ
Greek Alphabet

The Flood	792 Years	Exodus
1656		2448

In order to spread the gospel, the early church fathers (Lactantius and several others) started researching history books that were already very ancient in their time. These included the history books of Herodotus, Strabo, Sanchoniathon, Ennius and others. The church fathers discovered the "gods" were simply deified men. The fathers identified where the "gods" actually ruled, died, and where they were buried. This evidence proved the Greek/Roman religion was false. Ultimately, the Roman Empire became Christian. Here is a brief synopsis of what they discovered:

The sons of Javan, son of Japheth, settled in Greece. The modern Hebrew word for Greece is still Javan. When they began to settle, they had no king ruling over them, and still worshiped the one true God.

In the course of time, some of the sons of Gomer migrated from the area around ancient Scythia up to the area of the Black Sea. (See the chapter on Ancient Ireland for more detail on Scythia.) After a few skirmishes they controlled Cappadocia and Pontus. One of these princes was named Maneus. Maneus settled down and built two cities. One was located on the Black Sea. It was called Acmonia,

81

named after his son, and one called Themicyra, named after his daughter. Themicyra was located near the river Thermodon.

Maneus, Acmon, and Uranus

Maneus' son, Acmon, became consumed with a desire for conquest. Leaving the Black Sea area, he and his brother Doeas led an expedition into upper Phrygia. They began to refer to themselves as Titans. Acmon took the title of "Most High," and required all his conquered peoples to sacrifice and make oblation to him. We could say "the gods" were born in Phrygia. Using Phrygia as a base of operations, their power extended further into Greece, and eventually, Italy. Acmon's son was named Uranus/Coelus. Uranus was a man of science. Although he took the title of "prince," he did not think of himself as a god. It is said that Uranus died in Oceania and was buried in the town of Aulatia.

Saturn

Among the sons of Uranus were Titan and Saturn/Kronos. Saturn's older brother, Titan, wanted to rule the kingdom, but his mother and two sisters (Ceres) supported his brother Saturn to be the next ruler. Titan made an agreement with his brother, Saturn. He would allow Saturn to take the throne under two conditions: first, that he had no male heirs, and second, at his death one of Titan's sons would be ruler in his place. An Oracle prophesied that Saturn would have a son that would overthrow Saturn's kingdom. So Saturn sacrificed all of his sons to "the gods." He is also said to have castrated his father to prevent further rivals for the throne. Saturn married Rhea, one of his sisters, who Uranus had secretly sent to kill Saturn. Saturn seized several of Uranus' providences, and in the end captured and confined Uranus. Uranus died in grief.

Under Saturn's rule his kingdom reached from Syria and Phoenicia all the way to Spain and Mauritania in Africa.

Belus

Belus, who was deified and worshiped by Babylonians and Assyrians, ruled Babylon at the same time in history as Saturn ruled in Greece. This was about 322 years before the great Trojan War.

Jupiter

When Saturn's wife became pregnant again, she arranged to travel to Arcadia, so if she had a son, he might not be sacrificed as the others were. Saturn's son Jupiter/Zeus/Zen was born in Arcadia. He was sent to Mt. Ida on the Island of Crete to be hidden from Saturn. Named Jupiter, the boy was raised by Melisseus, king of the Cretans, as his own son. Melisseus was the first king in Crete who sacrificed to the gods. Melisseus appointed his daughter Melissa to be the first priestess of the "Great Mother." Later, when Titan learned that Saturn had sons, thus breaking the agreement between them, he and his sons, known as the Titans, took Saturn prisoner, sealing him and his wife Ops/Vesta into a wall. Jupiter then assembled a small army from Crete and took the kingdom back, restoring his father to the throne. Saturn, however, now knew he had a son. Because of the oracle's prophecy that his own son would destroy him, he set up an ambush to kill Jupiter. Saturn assumed that those to whom he had entrusted the government of Crete would still be loyal to him. He led a small band of warriors into Crete, but Jupiter was ready for him, having turned the government to his side. Saturn fled to that part of Greece called Peloponesus. Jupiter pursued his father to Peloponesus; so Saturn fled further to Italy. When the Titans of some other provinces learned that Jupiter had dethroned Saturn and was determined to take over the empire, they formed a confederacy against him. Jupiter went as far as Spain to end the war. The last great battle was fought near the coastal city of Tartesa, a little north of Cadiz. Saturn later died and was buried on the island of Sicily. His tomb was still being shown in the third century AD, according to church father Cyprian. The War between Jupiter and Saturn lasted about ten years, which occurred "some years before the death of Abraham." After driving out Saturn, Jupiter violated his sisters, and married one. He was well known for his many adulteries and his practice of violating young boys.

If the war between Jupiter and Saturn, which lasted ten years, was in the last half of Abraham's life, then the ten-year period can be dated between 2048 and 2123 AM. I believe it is probably closer to the 2123 date.

Jupiter divided the kingdom by lot among himself and two other brothers, Neptune/Poseidon, and Pluto, who had also escaped Saturn's sacrifices. The empire of the east fell to Jupiter. A portion of the west fell to Pluto, whose surname was Agesilaus. The maritime coast, together with the islands, fell to Neptune. Ennius' history records many of the triumphs of King Jupiter. Jupiter set up temples in many countries to form alliances with those countries. Jupiter created a golden column in the Triphylian Temple chronicling all his triumphs. Jupiter's tomb is in Crete, on the north side of the city of Knossos. Knossos was supposed to have been founded by Vesta, his mother. The inscription over the tomb of Jupiter says in Greek "Zan Kronou" which means "Zeus, son of Kronos."

Hercules
Hercules was one of the sons of Jupiter/Zeus. He was known for his temper. When he arrived on the island of Rhodes he asked a plowman for one of his oxen to kill and

eat. When the plowman refused, Hercules killed both the oxen, and cursed the plowman. This is how cursing became a prominent component in the rites of Hercules on the Isle of Rhodes. When Hercules discovered that the rites of Saturn, as practiced on the island of Sicily, involved human sacrifice, he went there to put a stop to it. Hercules died and was buried in Cadiz, Spain. The straits of Gibraltar were originally called the Pillars of Hercules.

Other notes
At different times both the worship of Saturn and the worship of Jupiter involved human sacrifice. Jupiter visited oracles, proving he could not see into the future. He named the sky after his grandfather Uranus; built altars, and later sacrificed victims (whole burnt offerings) to the sky as a god. He must not have been a god himself. Jupiter's tomb was still well-known and visited in AD 250, according to church father Cyprian.

Venus was a princess on the island of Cypress, but she was also a very lewd woman. She taught the women of Cypress to practice prostitution as a means of gain. One can see how she could be worshiped as the "goddess of love."

Witnessing
What we should take from this history is that, as Christians, we need to find the truth behind the myths and legends of false religions and cults. The church fathers dug up all this history from books already ancient in their time. They wanted to show from the sacred texts of the Greeks and Romans that their gods are simply deified men. Why worship what you know are not gods but just dead men?

This information helped Christians take over the pagan Roman Empire. We can use the same method today. If we expose the real history behind the false religions and cults from their own "sacred" texts, we will have a stronger chance to convert unbelievers.

Note on Horoscopes:

The modern horoscope is yet another example of a demonic trap. Astrology is based on the idea that the position of the planets on a given day compared to where they were when you were born, can predict your future. For instance: if Mars is in a certain position, I will have strife at work; or if Venus is in another position, my love life will improve. We know this is based on Greek and Roman myths of Mars being the god of War and Venus being the goddess of Love.

Astrology is based on gods and goddesses who were just men and women who are long since dead and buried. Doesn't that mean that modern astrology is a joke? Knowing this instantly frees us from being enslaved to it!

Church Father Tatian said it best,

> "Demons invented the concept of fate with astrology to enslave man into worshiping them."
> *Tatian to the Greeks 9*

Jupiter and Cilix

The historian Euemerus records that Jupiter, at the height of his power, traveled to Arabia and Babylon. He was warmly greeted by Bel, the ruler the Babylonians would later worship. He then went to the Island of Panchea somewhere in the Indian Ocean. (No one has ever located Panchea.) Jupiter erected massive temples to himself, Saturn, and Uranus. In each temple he recorded the deeds each did during their rule. Ennius, in his history, adds that Jupiter wrote all his triumphs on a golden pillar in the Triphylian Temple in Panchean characters. People have long sought this temple all over the Indian Ocean, including Sri Lanka. Today no one takes ancient history seriously, so few are even aware of the legend. Euemerus adds that Jupiter went through the area of Cilicia on his way back and conquered Cilix. Cilix was the brother of Europa and Cadmus, one of the many women Jupiter took advantage of.

Information taken from:
Church fathers Lactantius (DI 1.9-23), Tertullian (Gods of the Heathen), Arnobius (Against the Heathen) and Ancient historians Hesiod (Theognis), Apollodorus (Bibliotheca), Pezron (Antiquities of Nations), and Philocorus.

Chapter 13
Ireland and Scotland

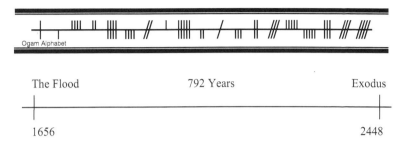

The Flood	792 Years	Exodus
1656		2448

Geoffrey Keating is one of very few Gaelic historians. Gaelic is one of the main languages spoken in Ireland. In ancient times Gaelic was written in the Ogam alphabet. In his work, *History of Ireland*, he dates Noah's flood at 1,656 years after creation. He uses several sources. His dates for the fall of the Tower of Babel and the Exodus are within six years of Jasher's dates for these events. Keating begins his story 140 years after the flood at 1796 AM. Here is a synopsis:

1796 AM
Adhna, son of Bioth, of the family of Nin, son of Bél first explored Ireland. He came to spy out the land, but did not stay long. He returned to his clan to give an account of Ireland, but he never returned.

1956 AM
Partholón, son of Sera, son of Sru, son of Esru, son of Fraimint, son of Fathacht, son of Magog, son of Japheth, son of Noah, was the first to occupy the island. Partholón came with Dealgnaid, his wife, and their three sons, Rudhruidhe, Slangha, and Laighlinne, with their wives, and a host of about a thousand. (One account says it was twenty-two years before Abraham was born; but another

says thirty years after his birth. Three hundred years after the flood Abraham would be eight years old.) The seventh year after Partholón occupied Ireland, the first man of his people died. His name was Feadha, son of Tortan, from whom is named Magh Feadha. The reason Partholón fled to Ireland is that while battling his brother over the kingdom, he killed his father and mother. Because of their murders he was driven completely out of the land. This is also why God sent a plague to wipe out all of his people from Ireland.

Neimheadh

About thirty years after Partholón's group was destroyed by the plague, Neimheadh son of Agnoman, son of Pamp, son of Tat, son of Seara, son of Srú, son of Easrú, son of Framant, son of Fathacht, son of Magog, son of Japheth, son of Noah, came to settle in Ireland. They arrived in thirty-four ships containing thirty persons each.

Formorians (Sea Thief)

A group of Hamites, fearing they could not win a war with the children of Shem (because of the curse placed on the sons of Canaan by Noah) left Canaan to find a place of their own. Sailing through the Mediterranean Sea, they came to Ireland. They lived on their ships and made a practice of raiding the costal towns. This is why they were called Formorians, which translates into "sea thief" or, as we call them, pirates. They plagued the costal communities for a long time.

Firbolg

Simeon Breac, son of Starn, son of Neimheadh, led a group of five thousand from bondage in Greece to Ireland, 217 years after Niemheadh landed there. This group was known as the Firbolgs. There is a great deal of information in Keating's work about the chieftains of the five thousand

89

and where they settled, the cities they built, and the wars they fought.

Tuatha Dé Danann

Iobath, son of Beothach, of the posterity of Niemheadh, left Ireland and journeyed back to Greece. When a war broke out between Syria and Athens, Iobath led his people, the Tuatha Dé Danann, into the war with Athens, fighting against Syria. When Syria defeated the Athenians, Iobath's forces retreated to Europe in fear and eventually returned to Ireland.

Feinius Farsaidh

Magog appointed Boath, son of Magog, son of Japheth, son of Noah, the first king of Scythia. When Boath passed the kingdom to his son, Feinius Farsaidh, Feinius started a school for the sciences. This school began in 1933 AM, about sixty years before the fall of the Tower of Babel. The original language was called "Gortighern," but the Latins called it "Lingua Humana." When the original language became seventy languages at the fall of the Tower of Babel, Feinius sent students to each language group for about seven years to thoroughly learn each language. Upon their return, he incorporated languages into his school. He originally taught the three principle languages of the world: Greek, Hebrew, and Latin. Later he added many other languages. Some say that because Eber refused to help build the Tower of Babel, he and his family alone retained the original language, which from that time forward was called "Hebrew," named after Eber.

Feinius' son, Niul, went from Babylonia to Egypt to set up a school of languages on the Red Sea. He married Scota, the daughter of a pharaoh. Scota gave birth to Gaedheal, after whom the Gaelic language is named. Gaedheal migrated to Ireland with his kindred and named his settlement after his mother's name: Scota. Later the name was changed to Scotland.

Witnessing tips:
Today there is a doctrine known as British Israelism. British Israelism teaches the Jews are no longer God's chosen people and they have been replaced by the Celtic peoples of England, Ireland, and America. Keating's historical research clearly shows most of British Israelism is very mixed-up history. This information can be used to stop this kind of anti-semitism.

We do not know where the majority of the ten tribes are, so they may or may not be intermingled with the Celtic tribes. However, several doctrines of the British Israelite movement are in error. Some have become cultic.

1. The doctrine that the church (or the British) are the true ten tribes with all the blessings given to Israel has spread into the doctrine that the Jews in Israel today are rejected by God or are not really Jews at all.

   a. The *Protocols of the Elders of Zion* is a fake work pointing to a supposed conspiracy of Jews. This false document was used to start WWI. It was used again by the Nazis in WWII, by Sadam in the first Gulf War, and many other anti-Semitic groups.
   b. Daniel's timeline prophecy records that the "true" Jews must return to their land in AD 1948. Therefore, whichever group is in power in Israel at the present time have to be the "true" Jews.

The chart on the following page identifies just a few British Israelite errors, along with the historical facts presented in this book. These can be used as a witnessing tool to bring people out of British Israelite and neo-Nazi cults.

Symbols

The Triquetra, is a very ancient symbol. Recently it has been used as a symbol for Wicca. In the early days of Celtic Christianity, it was a symbol for the Trinity. We still see it used on the cover of some NKJV Bibles. Before the start of Christianity it had several pagan and secular meanings. In ancient times it was the symbol that all races were brothers through Noah and his three sons. This is why I chose to use the Triquetra as a chapter divider.

Another example of ancient symbols being perverted in modern times is the rainbow. Recently the rainbow has been used as a symbol of the New Age Movement. In ancient times it was a symbol of the Noahide covenant. (See chapter 4 for information on the seven Noahide laws.)

Remember, all things go back to God. As Christians, we should take back the ancient symbols and use them to teach truth!

British Israelite Errors

Error	Fact
Dardanus, who founded Troy, was descended from an Israelite king. (the Dara of 1 Chron 2:6; 1 Kings 4:31)	Dardanus was the son of Elisha, son of Javan, son of Japheth, son of Noah, according to several historical documents. Dardanus built Troy and named it after his son Troius.
Scotland was named after "Scota," the daughter of Zedekiah.	Scotland was named after "Scota" the daughter of Pharaoh Nectonibus when Niul married her and migrated to what is now Scotland.
The Tuatha De Danann are the lost tribe of Dan.	Tuatha De Danann were descended from Iobath, son of Beothach of the posterity of Neimheadh, son of Agnoman, son of Pamp, son of Tat, son of Seara, son of Srú, son of Easrú, son of Framant, son of Fathacht, son of Magog, son of Japheth, son of Noah.
Lia Fail or the "Stone of Destiny" was Jacob's pillar brought to Ireland by Jeremiah the prophet.	Lia Fail or the "Stone of Destiny" was brought to Ireland by the Tuatha De Danann about 500 to 700 after the Flood, or 1800 – 1600 BC, way before the Tribe of Dan left on ships.
Cadmus (Chalcol of 1 Chron 2:6; 1 Kings 4:31) who founded Athens and Thebes was an Israelite.	Cadmus was a descendant of the kings of Tyre, who in turn descended from the kings of Sidon. Sidon was settled by Zidon, the firstborn son of Canaan, son of Ham, son of Noah.
The Lacedemonians (or Spartans) were descendants of Abraham and therefore heirs to the promise.	They may have been descendants of Abraham through Keturah not Sarah. Josephus 12.4.10 & 1 Maccabees 12

Ancient Post-Flood History

Error	Fact
Danaus, founder of Argos, was an Israelite prince who did not migrate with Moses to the promised land. The descendants of Danus were called Danai.	Danaus left Egypt and came to Argos (Argives) 393 years before Moses led the Exodus from Egypt. (Josephus AP 1.15) The Danai were not connected with the Israelite tribe of Dan.

Information taken from:
The History of Ireland (BOOK I-II), by Geoffrey Keating; Saltair of Caiseal; Nennius; Book of Invasions; Dialogue of the Ancients

Chapter 14
Italy

ABCDEFGHIJKLMNOPQRSTUVWXYZ
Latin Alphabet

The Flood	792 Years	Exodus
1656		2448

The most ancient history of Italy records that Sabinah, the grandson of Tubal, settled in Italy, founded a city, and named it after himself. Some time afterwards, Chittim (or Rome) was founded. In order for Rome to grow quickly, a decree was issued that any criminal that would come to help colonize Rome would be declared a free man and made a citizen of Rome. This attracted a lot of criminals and caused the sons of Tubal not to intermarry or trade with them. Contrary to this written history, secular Italian history has theorized that a tribe called the Sabini came from the Adriatic coast; possibly speaking a language called Oscan, and settled on the western cost of Italy.

Rape of the Sabines
In 2039 AM, when Abraham was 91 years old, 383 years after Noah's flood, the Romans decided that since they could not trade or intermarry with the children of Tubal, they would secretly slip into their cities and steal as many of the young women as they could. They then took the women back to Rome. Tubal's children gathered forces and started a war to free their daughters. The war lasted eight years. By 2047 AM, just fifty-four years after the fall of the Tower of Babel, the Sabine daughters all had children of their own. The Romans stated if the Sabines

95

did not stop the besiegement of Rome they would put their own daughters and grandchildren on the front lines. Like it or not, they were all now related. So Tubal's children had no choice but to end the war and return home. This event is referred to in secular history as "the Rape of the Sabines."

Israel, Edom, Africa, and Italy

In the year 2255 AM, seventeen years after the children of Israel migrated into Egypt, Jacob died at the age of 147. He commanded his children to take his body back to Canaan and bury it in the cave of Machpelah with Abraham, his father.

Esau heard of this and tried to prevent it, claiming Jacob had no right to be buried there. The sons of Esau attacked Joseph and his men at the cave. Joseph, his brothers, and the Egyptians with them, fought back and Chushim, son of Dan, son of Jacob, beheaded Esau (Jasher 56).

Zepho

Zepho, son of Eliphaz, son of Esau, swore revenge on Joseph for the death of his grandfather. He mounted a counterattack even before Joseph was back in Egypt. Zepho's forces were quickly defeated and he was captured and taken back to Egypt as a prisoner.

Esau's sons took Esau's body to Mt. Seir and buried it there. Afterwards, a coalition of the children of Esau, the people of Seir, together with the children of the east, went to Egypt to make war with Joseph and the Egyptians at the city of Raamses to free Zepho. They were again defeated. Then the Seirites demanded that the sons of Esau leave Seir and go back to Canaan but they refused. Thus the Seirites and the children of the east, together with Midian, came against the children of Esau. The children of Easu, together with reinforcements from Angeas, king of Africa, fought with them in the wilderness of Paran. The Seirites were wiped out and the rest fled. The sons of Esau took possession of the land of Seir and became known as Edomites (Jasher 57).

In 2270 AM, thirty-two years after the children of Israel migrated into Egypt, Magron became Pharaoh. He placed Joseph, who was seventy-one years old and had been ruling as vice-pharaoh for forty-one years, in complete control of all of Egypt. Joseph ruled in total authority for forty years until his death at the age of one hundred and ten. During this time he subdued the Philistines, all of Canaan with Zidon, and the other side of the Jordan. He collected yearly tribute from all of them.

In 2288 AM, the Edomites, along with the children of the east, the children of Ishmael, and forces from Angeas of Africa, attacked Joseph at Raamses. Joseph again defeated them (Jasher 58).

In 2309 AM, Joseph died at one hundred and ten years of age, seventy-one years after the children of Israel migrated into Egypt. Rulership reverted to the pharaohs. In 2310 AM, Zepho escaped Egypt, fleeing to Angeas king of Africa. Angeas made Zepho captain of his host. Zepho tried unsuccessfully to convince Angeas to attack Egypt (Jasher 59).

Zepho left Africa and went to Rome. He led many successful battles for Rome and eventually was crowned king. Zepho then subdued Italy and the surrounding islands, creating the first unified Italy. He reigned over the newly created Roman Empire for fifty years (Jasher 61).

The beginning of this united Roman Empire took place about 1400 years before Christ.

Date	Edomite Kings and years reigned	Reference
	Esau	
	Eliphaz	
2248-2278	Bela (30)	Jasher 57
2288-2297	Jobab (10)	Jasher 58
2297-2317	Chusam (20)	
2317-2363	Hadad (46)	Jasher 66
2363-2383	Salmah (18)	Jasher 66
2383-2423	Saul (40)	Jasher 69
2423-2446	Baal Channan (23)	Jasher 74
2446-2494	Hadad (48)	Jasher 78
2494-	Abianus of Rome conquers Edom	Jasher 90

Date	Roman Kings and years reigned	Reference
	Uzu?	
2317-2367	Zepho (50)	Jasher 60
2367-2417	Janeas (50)	Jasher 67
2417-2462	Latanus (45)	Jasher 74
~2435	Alba made capital of the Empire	
2462-2500	Abianus (38)	Jasher 84
2500-2550	Latinus II (50)	Jasher 90
~2855	Capital moved to Rome	

Date	African Kings and years reigned	Reference
????-2411	Angeas (>156)	Jasher 74
2411-2411	Azdrubal	Jasher 74
2411-????	Anibal	Jasher 74

In 2340 AM, Angeas sent a raiding fleet to Rome, only to have it destroyed by Zepho. Angeas sent for help from his brother Lucas, king of Sardinia, and together they battled Rome. Edom refused to help Rome. With defeat imminent, Zepho prayed to the God of Abraham asking Him to remember His covenant with all of Abraham's sons. God harkened to Zepho's prayers and delivered Rome from Angeas. (Jasher 63)

Zepho forsook the God of his Father Abraham and mustered the forces of Rome, Edom, the children of Ishmael, and the children of the east to attack Israel and Egypt. In the first wave, the Egyptian outposts were destroyed. The Israelites joined with the Egyptians and destroyed the invaders. Upon finding out that some of the Egyptian forces fled during battle, the Israelites fell upon the fleeing Egyptians and killed them. (Jasher 64)

As a result, all of Egypt feared Israel. Pharaoh Melol came up with a plan to "refortify" Pithom and Raamses. The Egyptians and Israelites gladly undertook the project. Slowly the Egyptians withdrew and enslaved the Israelites. (Jasher 65)

In 2363 AM, the thirteenth year of the reign of Pharaoh Menrenre Antiemsaf I, one hundred and twenty-five years after the children of Israel migrated into Egypt, Edom resolved to attack Rome, to avenge the destruction of Angeas' army. At the last moment they turned back. Menrenre ruled a total of fourteen years, and was apparently co-ruling with Pepi II who took the throne at the age of six (Jasher 66). See Sixth Dynasty chart in the chapter on Egypt.

In 2420 AM, the third year of his reign, Latinus attacked Africa. Latinus killed Azdrubal and took Azdrubal's sister as a bride. Angeas' second son, Anibal, took the throne of Africa. Anibal went to war with Rome, to avenge his brother; he occupied Rome for eighteen years. This occurred from 2420-2438 AM (Jasher 74)

In 2494 AM, the Roman King Abianus went to war and subdued all of Edom. Edom remained under the control of Rome many years (Jasher 90).

Latinus II became king of Rome in 2500 AM. During his reign, he conquered Brittania, Kernania, and the Greeks, (children of Elisha, son of Javan). Edom rebelled during this war but Latinus quickly regained control of Edom.

Three Hannibals

Three *different* Hannibals attacked Rome from Africa/Carthage. The first Anibal (or Hannibal) was the son of Angeas, who lived about 1400 BC. The second was a general named after him approximately five hundred years later. The third and most famous, was the general Hannibal, who in the 220's BC, attacked Rome from Carthage and was defeated by the Roman general, Scipio.

From Alba to Rome

Church father Arnobius (A.H. 2.71) used Italian history that came from ancient Roman historical records. These agree with the Jasher scroll, but add the following:

From the time of Zeus to Latinus I was approximately 320 years. The original capital of the Roman Empire was the town of Alba. Alba was founded by Anibal during his eighteen-year occupation of Italy. The kings of Italy ruled from Alba for about 420 years. The capital was then moved to the city of Rome. Arnobius reports that from the time the city of Rome was made the capital, to the birth of Christ was about 1050 years. *1050 years to Christ*

Jasher wrote that Latinus took the throne in 2417 AM, or approximately 1508 BC. The 1050 + 420 years later would put us at 38 BC, within forty years of the birth of Christ. We were told Abraham was still alive during the war between Zeus and Saturn. Notice 320 years back from 1508 BC is 1828 BC, which is in the lifetime of Father Abraham.

Remus and Romulus

In Roman myth, Rome was founded by Remus and Romulus, who as children were nursed by a she-wolf. This is a good example of real history being reinterpreted by pagans. As we have learned, Zepho, grandson of Esau, pulled together the city states and founded the first united Italy. He then trained and handed over the government to the first Latin king. In ancient Latin "Zepho" can be translated "she-wolf."

So the she-wolf myth is an ancient memory corrupted by pagans and a testimony to the accuracy of ancient Hebrew history! The first kings of the Roman Empire (not the city of Rome) were nursed (trained by) the she-wolf (Zepho).

Facts taken from:
Arnobius, *Against the Heathen*; *Book of Jasher*; and Lactantius, *Divine Institutes*.

Chapter 15
Russia

АБВГДЕЖЗИЙКЛМНОПТУФХЦЧЩЪЬЭЮЯ
Russian Alphabet

The Ancient land of Scythia is now called southern Russia. This land extended north from the Caucasus Mountains to the west as far as Kazakhstan, and to the east as far as the Ukraine.

> "Now these are the generations of the sons of Noah, Shem, Ham, and Japheth: and unto them were sons born after the flood. The sons of Japheth; Gomer, and Magog, and Madai, and Javan, and Tubal, and Meshech, and Tiras." *Genesis 10:1-2 KJV*

Josephus, in *Antiquities of the Jews 1.6*, wrote the descendants of Magog settled north of the Caucasus Mountains and the Black Sea and they were called Scythians by the Greeks.

> "Magog founded those that from him were named Magogites, but who are by the Greeks called Scythians." *Josephus Ant. 1.6.1*

According to *Historia Regum Britanniae*, written by Irish historian Geoffrey of Monmouth, Magog crowned his firstborn son, Boath, the first king of Scythia. In time Boath

Scythian Kings
Magog
Boath
Feinius Farsa

turned the kingdom over to his first-born son, Feinius Farsa. Notice the difference in the names. You can tell the Tower of Babel had fallen and the languages had been created before Feinius took the throne.

For full details on Feinius' School and his descendants forming the country of Scotland, see the chapter on Ireland.

Jasher indicates some of the sons of Meshach and Tiras settled in the areas of southern Russia and Mongolia.

"And the children of Meshech are the Shibashni and the children of Tiras are Rushash, Cushni, and Ongolis; all

Ongolis	=	Mongolia
Cura River	=	Sura River
Tragan River	=	Volga River
Jabus Sea	=	Caspian Sea
Me'at	=	Arctic Ocean

these went and built themselves cities; those are the cities that are situated by the sea Jabus by the river Cura, which empties itself in the river Tragan." *Jasher 10:14*

"Magog [dwells in] all the inner portions of the north until it reaches to the sea of Me'at."
Jubilees 9:9

Moscow is on the Moskva River which empties into the Volga (Tragan) River.

It should also be noted that some of the sons of Meshech and Tubal settled in the areas of Greece and Italy. The sons of Magog, Tubal, Meshech, and Tiras are as follows:

"And the sons of Magog were Elichanaf and Lubal." *Jasher 7:4*

"And the sons of Tubal were Ariphi, Kesed and Taari. And the sons of Meshech were Dedon, Zaron and Shebashni. And the sons of Tiras were Benib, Gera, Lupirion and Gilak;" *Jasher 7:1-9*

So, modern Russians are descended from Magog.

Ezekiel 38-39

Ezekiel records a prophecy about Russia and her allies invading Israel. Now we know which modern countries these ancient Hebrew names refer to.

> "Son of man, set your face toward Gog of the land of Magog, the prince of Rosh, Meshech and Tubal, and prophesy against him." *Ezekiel 38:2 NASB*

> "Persia, Ethiopia and Put with them, all of them with shield and helmet; Gomer with all its troops; Beth-togarmah from the remote parts of the north with all its troops--many peoples with you." *Ezekiel 38:5-6 NASB*

As mentioned elsewhere in this book, Persia is modern Iran, ancient Ethiopia is the area of modern Ethiopia and Sudan, Put is modern Libya, Gomer is modern Germany, all of Germany's troops or parts would include Austria. Beth-Togarmah, or the house of Togarmah, would include not only Georgia, and Armenia, but also Turkey.

For details on which part of this prophecy has already been fulfilled and what part is yet to come, see *Ancient Prophecies Revealed.*

Chapter 16
Troy

Theban Alphabet

The Flood	792 Years	Exodus
1656		Angeas dies 2448

We learned from the chapter on Greece that the descendants of Magog conquered the Greek city states and began to be worshiped as gods.

Africa

The first inhabitants of northern Africa (called Libya at the time) were nomads and anarchists. They rejected any authority or form of government. Josephus wrote that about the time Hercules ruled Greece, two grandsons of Abraham by Keturah, named Aphra, (whom the continent of Africa was named after) and Japbran, joined the war with Hercules against Libya, in order to subdue the natives (Troglodytes) and form a lasting government. Josephus wrote that Hercules actually married Abraham's great-grand daughter!

> "Hercules married Aphra's daughter, and of her he begat a son, Diodorus; and that Sophon was his son, from whom that barbarous people called Sophacians were denominated."
> *Josephus Ant 1.15*

After the Libyan war ended, governments were set up and the Libyans (Africans) prospered. About this time Angeas survived the Trojan War and settled in Dinhabah, (also called Annaba, a valley about fourteen miles from where the city of Carthage would be built).

Troy

The famous city of Troy was built by Dardanus, son of Flissa, son of Juuin, son of Japheth, son of Noah. He named the city after his son Troius. (Since Nennius corrupts Javan to Juuin and Elisha to Flissa, Dardanus was partially Greek.)

The great-great-grandson of Troius was the famous Trojan warrior Aeneas (called Angeas by Jasher). The great-grandson of Aeneas was Brutus. That makes nine generations from Noah to Aeneas, and twelve generations from Noah to Brutus. The only reliable date we seem to have is the death of Angeas at 2411 AM, just thirty-seven years before Moses led the Exodus from Egypt. Based on the date of the war between Zeus and Saturn (see the chapter on ancient Greece) and Angeas' death, we can place the destruction of Troy between 2123 and 2411 AM.

Agamemnon, great-grandson of Zeus, ruled Greece and launched the ships that destroyed Troy. The Trojan warrior Aeneas, after escaping the great Trojan War, began to assemble the mighty African empire.

It is said that Brutus led his brethren out of slavery in Greece to Brittan, where he founded the city of New Troy, later renamed London.

Angeas king of Africa

We first encounter Angeas in Jasher 57. At the time of Jacob's death, in 2255 AM, Angeas was already king of Africa. This means he lived longer than 156 years. His

African kingdom extended from the shores of Libya (northern Africa bordering on the Mediterranean Sea) to Italy. Parts of Italy and Greece were included in his kingdom from time to time.

Aeneas and Turnus
Perhaps one of the most famous battles of ancient times was the battle between Aeneas and Turnus. I(zu) a great governor of a provenience in Italy, (later worshiped as a Roman god) had a beautiful daughter named Jania. Angeas asked for and was promised her hand in marriage. Turnus of Rutuli, also wanting her as a wife and finding he could not have the marriage promise broken, made war against Aeneas. Aeneas killed Turnus and took Jania as his bride (Jasher 60).

This historical information is supported by Roman historian Livy and the poet Virgil.

Inaccurate Greek, Roman, and Egyptian history
Most of Greek and Roman history comes from epic poems like the Aeneid and the Odyssey. These are like today's Hollywood movies. They were never meant to be used as history guides. For instance, in epic poems we have Aeneas in a steamy love affair with princess Elissa, but as all historians know this could not have occurred.

Josephus gives an account of the chronology from Tyrian records showing the dedication of Solomon's temple was exactly 143 years before the time princess Elissa left Tyre and founded Carthage at about 850 BC. Solomon's temple was dedicated at 2935 AM. Adding 2935 to 143 brings us to 3078 AM. Aeneas death was 2411 AM, which is a difference of 667 years! This is a little too far apart to have a romance. *2935*

Other examples of secular historians confusing history are:

Ceops (meaning "lord of light") created the great pyramid. The name exists in pre-Flood king lists and the fourth dynasty Egyptian king list. This pre-Flood monument's history is credited to the wrong Ceops.

In the third Egyptian dynasty we have two Djosers. According to Jasher's chronology, the *second* Djoser lived during the period when Joseph/Imhotep created the step pyramid and the Egyptian famine occurred. Most credit the first Djoser with these.

Egyptian history reads as though the dynasties were consecutive. This would put creation at 7000 BC, which is not possible according to the Bible.

Many examples like these are given by ancient historians demonstrating why Greek, Roman, and Egyptian histories are not to be fully trusted. These same ancient historians credit Tyrian, Babylonian (Berosus), Hebrew, and Syrian histories as being highly accurate.

Information taken from:
Cory's Ancient Fragments, Geoffrey of Monmouth's *History of Ireland*, Nennius's *History of Britian*, Josephus' *Antiquities of the Jews*, and the *Book of Jasher*.

Shem's Descendants

Arab Nations
China
India
Iran
Iraq / Babylon
Israel
Kurds

Chapter 17
Arab Nations

ح أ ذ ر ز ب ب ب ب ب ب ت ث ت ث ك س س ص ص ص ط ط ظ ظ ن م ذ ل كم
Arabic Alphabet

Modern Arabs trace their descent through Ishmael, Abraham's son by Hagar, or through the sons of Abraham and Keturah.

Ishmael was the son of Abraham and Hagar. He was born in Mamre when Abraham was 86, in the Hebrew year 2034 AM. He died at the age of 137 in the year 2472 AM.

> "And these are the years of the life of Ishmael, an hundred and thirty and seven years: and he gave up the ghost and died; and was gathered unto his people." *Genesis 25:17.*

During Ishmael's life, God promised to make him a great nation in answer to Abraham's prayer (Genesis 17:18, 20).

> "And God was with the lad; and he grew, and dwelt in the wilderness, and became an archer. And he dwelt in the wilderness of Paran: and his mother took him a wife out of the land of Egypt." *Genesis 21:20-21*

Ishmael's first wife was an Egyptian named Rebah (Meribah). She bore Ishmael four sons and one daughter, named Bosmath. Meribah was not a good wife and at the insistence of father Abraham, Ishmael put her away. Ishmael married again. Father Abraham approved Ishmael's second wife, Malchuth (Faṭimah). See Jasher 53.

"These are their genealogies: the firstborn of Ishmael was Nebaioth, then Kedar, Adbeel, Mibsam, Mishma, Dumah, Massa, Hadad, Tema, Jetur, Naphish and Kedemah; these were the sons of Ishmael. The sons of Keturah, Abraham's concubine, whom she bore, were Zimran, Jokshan, Medan, Midian, Ishbak and Shuah. And the sons of Jokshan were Sheba and Dedan."
1 Chronicles 1:29-32

The Sons and Grandsons of Ishmael

Rebah's sons	Grandsons
Nebaioth	Mend, Send, Mayon
Kedar	Alyon, Kezem, Chamad, Eli
Adbeel	Chamad, Jabin
Mibsam	Obadiah, Ebedmelech, Yeush

Malchuth's sons	Grandsons
Nishma	Shamua, Zecaryon, Obed
Dumah	Kezed, Eli, Machmad, Amed
Massa	Melon, Mula, Ebidadon
Hadad	Azur, Minzar, Ebedmelech
Tema	Seir, Sadon, Yakol
Yetur	Merith, Yaish, Alyo, Pachoth
Naphish	Ebed-Tamed, Abiyasaph, Mir
Kedemah	Kedma, Calip, Tachti, Omir

Jasher 53

"Then again Abraham took a wife, and her name was Keturah. And she bare him Zimran, and Jokshan, and Medan, and Midian, and Ishbak, and Shuah. And Jokshan begat Sheba, and Dedan. And the sons of Dedan were Asshurim, and Letushim, and Leummim. And the sons of Midian; Ephah,

and Epher, and Hanoch, and Abidah, and Eldaah. All these were the children of Keturah."
Genesis 25:1-4

The Sons and Grandsons of Abraham and Keturah	
Sons	Grandsons
Zimran	Abihen, Molich, Narim
Jokshan	Sheba and Dedan
Medan	Amida, Joab, Gochi, Elisha, Nothach
Midian	Ephah, Epher, Chanoch, Abida, Eldaah
Ishbak	Makiro, Beyodua, Tator
Shuach	Bildad, Mamdad, Munan, Meban

Jasher 53

Sheba and Dedan are ancient cities on the Red Sea coast of Saudi Arabia. Midian fathered the Midianites. Josephus connects Nebaioth with the Nabataeans.

The Bible prophesies that the Arabs would always be against Israel and each other. This prophecy was given almost 2,000 years before the rise of Islam.

"And he will be a wild man; his hand will be against every man, and every man's hand against him; and he shall dwell in the presence of all his brethren." *Genesis 16:12*

The Arab peoples mainly occupy the countries of Jordan, Bahrain, Kuwait, Oman, Qatar, Saudi Arabia, the United Arab Emirates, and Yemen.

Chapter 18
China

丰业么丛乏东万下三专之丽乒乏丁个不丐丢丞
Chinese Writing

The Flood	792 Years	Exodus

1656   Xia   ToB   Shang   2448

Secular historians identify the first recorded Chinese Dynasty as the Xia Dynasty (or the Hsia Dynasty) which dates from about 2100 to 1700 BC. The Xia Dynasty was replaced by the Shang dynasty dating from 1700 to 1127 BC. This would place the beginning of Xia Dynasty about one hundred and fifty years after the Flood, and ending about fifty years after the death of Shem, son of Noah.

150 years After Flood

The first *written* Chinese history appears in the Shang Dynasty, about 200 years after the fall of the Tower of Babel. It is abreviated "ToB" in the chart above.

The most ancient histories describe how the "Yellow Emperor," led his people from Mesopotamia to the Yellow River area in China.

Border Sacrifice
In Beijing, China, there is a place called "the Temple of Heaven," built about AD 1500. It was the center of the worship of ShangDi or "Heavenly Ruler." The worship of ShangDi included a "border sacrifice."

At each New Year's ceremony, the emperor sacrificed a bull on the great white marble Altar of Heaven. They

113

invoked the aid of the Creator of the universe to grant wisdom to the emperor to govern the people in the following year.

This sacrifice is similar to the animal sacrifices Noah and the patriarchs made to the one true God and parallels the Jewish High Priest sacrificing the bull during the once-per-year ceremony of Yom Kippur. There were no idols in the temple of ShangDi.

According to Confucius' Shu Jing or "Book of History," Shun, founder of the Xia Dynasty, offered border sacrifices to ShangDi. This makes the border sacrifice of ShangDi over 4000 years old! After the last border sacrifice, performed in 1911 AD, the communists deposed the last Emperor of China.

Who is ShangDi?
The English translation of the Chinese ShangDi, or ShangTi, is "heavenly ruler." In the mythic history of the Xia Dynasty we learn that Pangu (or ShangDi) the Creator of the universe, created the first man. From him came a succession of legendary sage leaders, ending in Yu. The Miao people, who lived in southern China, say Yu, the tenth generation from Creation, created a ship to survive a great flood. All peoples who now exist are descended from Yu.

We also have the legends of the "Three August Ones" and "Five Emperors" that existed before Shun, the founder of the Xia Dynasty.

The "Three August Ones" were god-kings who had magical powers and lived exceedingly long lives. Their names were Fuxi (伏羲), Nüwa (女娲), and Shennong (神

農 .) According to legend, Fuxi and Nuwa were the husband and wife god and goddess who created all mankind. Notice that in Chinese history, Nuwa was the *mother* of mankind while in the Bible, Noah is the *father* of mankind.

The third "August One" was Shennong. His full title is 炎帝神农氏, which translates to "The Yellow Emperor and patriarch, Shennong." He was supposed to be the founder of the Chinese people. He was also credited with identifying hundreds of medicinal and poisonous plants. The book 神农本草经 (The Shennong Herb-Root Classic) is compiled from his writings. "Shennong" could be Shem, the son of Noah, who lived 500 years after the flood, or, perhaps, a descendant named after him.

Chinese history records God's Creation of the earth, the destruction of the Flood, Noah and Naamah as the parents of all mankind, and Shem. After them, apparently, came five emperors or kings from Shem to Shun who founded the first Chinese Dynasty.

Miautso Legends

The Miautso people of China are divided into eleven tribes which are said to be descended from a man named Seageweng. Seageweng was the son of Gangen Newang, who was the son of Jenku Dawvu. Jenku Dawvu was a descendant of Gawandan Mewwan who was the son of Tutan who was a descendant of Gomen (Gomer). Goman was the son of Lo Jahpu (Japheth) who was the son of Nuah (Noah). Nuah survived the great flood in a large boat. Other sons of Nuah were Lo Han (Ham) and Lo Shen (Shem). Another part of the legend gives the names of the sons of Lo Han as Cusah (Cush) and Mesay (Mizriam) and the names of the sons of Shen as Elan (Elam) and Nga shur (Asshur).

Of the eleven Miautso tribes, six intermarried with other peoples who settled in the area forming the Chinese nation, while five remained a pure distinct people among the Chinese.

So we have several legends and written records tracing various ethnic peoples of China back to Shem and Japheth.

Information taken from:
Shu Jing by Confucius, *Records of the Grand Historian* by Sima Qian, *the Records of Yundou shu* (運斗樞), and the *Records of Yuanming bao* (元命苞).

Chapter 19
India

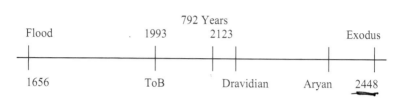

अब चदेङगहजिक लमहनख पटेरसतुव थधचयश रबय

Sanskrit Alphabet

```
                         792 Years
Flood              1993    2123                    Exodus
+--------------+---------+--+---------------+--------+
1656              ToB       Dravidian    Aryan   2448
```

The Guti were the first to begin driving out the Hamites from Babylonia. The Guti were the Bactrians, children of Gether, son of Aram, son of Shem. This happened immediately after the death of Nimrod, at 2123 AM. One group of Hamites fled to the area of the Copan River in India.

Josephus states the sons of Joctan, son of Eber, namely Elmodad, Saleph, Asermoth, Jera, Adoram, Aizel, Decla, Ebal, Abimael, Sabeus, Ophir, Euilat, and Jobab inhabited the land up to the Cophen River in India. These same Hamites were driven further into India by the sons of Joctan. They settled in the Indus valley and became known as the Dravidians. This is the start of the Vedic race.

Their religion was an outgrowth of the original false religion developed by Nimrod.

We have many of their writings; but, their language has never been deciphered.

117

A century or two later, a Japhetic race came down and intermarried with the Hamatic Dravidians. They brought with them the Aryan language, Sanskrit.

The oldest copy of the Rig Veda (a Hindu poem written in Sanskrit) is dated about the same time as the Exodus, 1450 BC. The difference between Nimrod's death at 2123 AM and the Exodus date of 2448 AM is 325 years. So the development of the Hindu Religion, as we know it, happened in only 325 years.

A legend among the Korean people says they were originally populated by the descendants of Joctan, son of Eber.

Hinduistic History

Even inside Hinduism there are memories of real history. Hinduism teaches that the earth has been destroyed many times. In the last destruction, a man named Satyavarata (also called Manu) built a ship and escaped a great flood, landing on Mt. Hivamet in northern India. (This is according to the Hindu poem Mahabarata.)

Babylonian Mystery Religion

The original pre-Flood apostasy started with the teaching that the creator God was an impersonal force, not a person to be feared and listened to. This impersonal force, along with other spirits/forces, can be manipulated by magic and astrology.

Hinduism and Wicca

Hinduism and Wicca are the purest and oldest forms of the Babylonian mystery religion. Both teach magic, astrology, multiple gods, evolution and reincarnation. Both teach the doctrine of "Emanation," which states that the energy of the original creator/force has emptied itself into man. Each man has a little piece of the creator/force in him. In Hinduism, this is called the "Atman." In Wicca, the concept is taught but it does not have a name.

The following chart contrasts the teachings of the great apostasy of the Babylonian mystery religion (see Genesis 10 & Revelation 17) with the true religion practiced by father Noah and the righteous patriarchs.

Babylonian Mystery Religion	The True Patriarchal Religion
1. Evolution	1. Special Creation
2. Reincarnation	2. Resurrection
3. Astrology	3. No Astrology
4. Many gods or idols	4. One true Creator (Trinity)
5. Original creator god is an impersonal force	5. Original creator God is a person
6. There is a piece of god in each of us	6. God is totally separate from His creation
7. Magic rites to manipulate the spirits/forces	7. Pray to God for answers

The Goddess Diana

In Acts 19:19, Paul instructs the new Ephesian Christian converts to burn their magic books. Archeology has unearthed some of these texts. Diana's magic rites included spells, amulets, and talismans invoking her for aid. Exactly the same thing is found in Hinduism and Wicca.

The following chart compares present day world religions and the teachings from the great apostasy:

	Mag	CEF	CNF	CEP	MG	Em	Re
Buddhism	✓		✓				✓
Confucianism	✓	✓					✓
Druidism	✓				✓		✓
Hinduism	✓	✓			✓	✓	✓
Jainism	✓			✓		✓	✓
Kabbalah	✓	✓			✓	✓	✓
Shamanism	✓				✓		✓
Shinto	✓	✓			✓		✓
Sikh	✓					✓	
Sufi	✓					✓	✓
Tao	✓	✓					✓
Voodoo	✓			✓	✓		
Wicca	✓		✓		✓	✓	✓
Zoroastrianism	✓			✓	✓		
Christianity				✓			
Islam				✓			
Judaism				✓			

Mag = Belief in Magic, **Re** = Reincarnation, **MG** = Multiple gods/creators, **CEF** = The Creator exists but is an impersonal force **CNF** = The Creator does not exist, but was an impersonal force **CEP** = The Creator exists and is a person **Em** = There is an Emanation of the original Creator God in each of us

Definitions:

Magic – The belief that there are rites we can perform to manipulate spirits to force them to do what we want them to. (Spirits may be called impersonal forces, in the case of an atheistic magician.)

Incantations and spells – Rituals preformed in order to achieve manipulation of said forces/spirits.

Amulets – A physical object of occult power that will protect the owner from something (perhaps evil spirits).

Talismans – A physical object of occult power that will cause something to happen (grant the owner peace, prosperity, or love.)

Astrology – The belief that the positions of the planets govern behavior and events.

Conclusion:
As the time of the great harlot church approaches, we must watch for any form of this Apostasy creeping into the church under different names. Evolution and reincarnation go hand-in-hand. With evolution already gaining great acceptance in many Christian churches, replacing the teaching of resurrection with reincarnation can't be far behind. The next point of apostasy will probably be the "I am a little god" concept, from the doctrine of Emanations.

For a complete discussion on the Preflood apostasy and the occult, inside and outside of the Church, see the book *Ancient Paganism*.

Information taken from:
Book of Jasher, Josephus' *Antiquities of the Jews*, and the Jewish *Talmud*.

Chapter 20
Iran

Persian Cuneiform Alphabet

The country today known as Iran was originally settled shortly after the Flood. Elam, the firstborn son of Shem, founded the Elamite Empire. The Elamites, along with many others, were overrun by Hamites when Nimrod seized control of Mesopotamia and founded the first post-Flood Babylonian Empire. The Elamites were enslaved from 1948-1993 AM, a total of forty-five or forty-six years. After the fall of the Tower of Babel, Chedolaomer became the leader of the Elamites, leading them back to independence. Eventually the Elamite Empire would be renamed the Persian Empire.

> "Shem, the third son of Noah, had five sons, who inhabited the land that began at Euphrates, and reached to the Indian Ocean. For Elam left behind him the Elamites, the ancestors of the Persians. Ashur lived at the city Nineve; and named his subjects Assyrians, who became the most fortunate nation, beyond others. Arphaxad named the Arphaxadites, who are now called Chaldeans. Aram had the Aramites, which the Greeks called Syrians." *Josephus 1.6.4*

During the first century BC, the Romans tried to conquer the Persians, which at that time were called Parthians by the Romans. The name Persia was finally replaced with Iran in AD 1935. It has been known as the Islamic Republic of Iran since 1979.

Ancient church father Julius Afracanus states in his work entitled *Narrative of Events Happening in Persia on the Birth of Christ*, written about AD 200, that pagan magi came from Persia to see the infant Jesus. He cites their written record about their experience meeting Mary and the baby Jesus. They even had artists with them that created a painting of the child Jesus on Mary's knee!

Future Events

Biblical prophecy states that Iran (Persia) would form a military pact with Russia (Magog). This took place in AD 2005. In the future, Iran, along with Russia, will invade the land of Israel. As a result, prophecy states that five-sixths of both countries (Iran and Russia) will be destroyed by fire.

Chapter 21
Iraq / Babylon

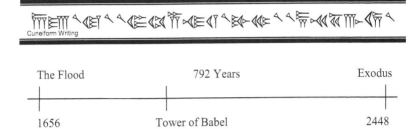
Cuneiform Writing

The Flood	792 Years	Exodus
1656	Tower of Babel	2448

As the children of Shem settled in the area of what is now called Syria and Iraq, one of the sons of Ham, Nimrod, invaded the land and created the first great Babylonian Empire. Secular history says Hammurabi formed the first great Babylonian Empire between 1950 and 1790 BC. The Persian records state he ruled forty-two years before the rebellion occurred that formed the Elamite Empire. Jasher has his reign last forty-five years.

Here is the story as given by Jasher and Josephus:

Nimrod
Nimrod, also called Amraphel and Hammurabi, was born in 1908 AM, 252 years after Noah's flood. He was the son of Cush, son of Ham, son of Noah. He built the cities of Babel, Erech, and Accad in Shinar. In Assyria, he built Nineveh and Calnah. God blessed Nimrod, allowing him to win all the wars he fought.

The Invasion
In 1948 AM, when Nimrod was forty, there was war between some of the sons of Japheth and his brethren. This was the same year Abraham was born. Nimrod assembled about 540 men and left Ethiopia to begin the invasion.

Each time he subdued a city state, like Ur, he would take the sons of that king captive with the understanding that any disobedience would result in the torture and death of that king's children.

After winning the war between the sons of Ham and the sons of Japheth, the sons of Ham in that area made Nimrod king over the people. Nimrod then built the city of Shinar and ruled from there.

The Empire Grows

During the next forty-five years, his empire flourished. Nimrod, with Chedorlaomer and the other kings, laid waste to all of Syria and subdued the offspring of the giants. Nimrod was called the "mighty hunter before the LORD" (LXX says Giant hunter). Nimrod wanted to have revenge on God for destroying his forefathers. He turned the government into a tyranny and set up twelve gods of wood corresponding to the twelve months of the year (or after the Zodiac), commanding everyone to worship one each month.

Tower of Babel

The Babylonians started construction on a massive tower in a valley two days' walk from Shinar. After working on the tower for a few years (not anywhere complete), God passed judgment on them. In 1993 AM, 337 years after the Flood, God changed the one language that all people spoke into seventy principle languages. Later, in time, these would sub-divide into the many languages we have today.

With all the confusion of the new languages, the people stopped building the city and the tower. A large portion of the tower was swallowed up in an earthquake. Abraham was forty-five years old when this happened.

The Elamite Empire
Within three years of the fall of the Tower of Babel, people dispersed by language into different parts of the world. Then one of the last of a series of major earthquakes occurred. This earthquake finished dividing the continents. Chedorlaomer then left the Babylonian Empire and formed the Elamite Empire (Persian) in Iran. After this, Nimrod finished building the city of Babel and constructed the cities of Erech, Accad, and Calnah.

Chedorlaomer's territory grew to include Sodom and Gomorrah. After being subject to Chedolaomer for twelve years, Sodom and Gomorrah rebelled and remained free for five years. In 2013 AM, Nimrod, seeing the cities remained free for five years, chose to make war with Chedorlaomer. By the end of the battle, Nimrod was defeated and his son, Mardon, who was more wicked than his father, was killed in the battle as well. In later Babylonian mythology, Mardon would be worshiped as the god Marduk.

Nimrod was under the subjection of Chedorlaomer for a long time, and this battle caused Tidal, king of Goyim, and Arioch, king of Elasar, to make a covenant with Chedorlaomer.

In 2034 AM, Chedorlaomer attacked the rebellious five cities with his collation of kings. Nimrod fought with the coalition of forces. After the fall of the Tower of Babel the people called Nimrod, Amraphel, which means "he who causes his people to fall." The cities of Sodom and Gomorrah were captured, along with Lot. Abraham attacked the collation of kings, freeing Lot and the kings of Sodom and Gomorrah. Abraham may have also killed Chedorlaomer in this battle.

From that time forward, Sodom and Gomorrah grew more and more wicked. In the Jewish year 2047 AM, God destroyed the cities by raining fire down on them. See the chapter on Sodom and Gomorrah for more details.

Nimrod's Death
In 2123 AM, Nimrod was 215 years old. This was just 467 years after the Flood.

Nimrod went hunting in his usual way. There had always been a rivalry between Nimrod and Esau as to who was the mightier hunter. Esau took the opportunity to behead Nimrod with a sword. This was the same year Abraham died. Esau, thinking he would be captured and executed, sold his birthright to Jacob. Instead of being hunted, everyone was relieved Nimrod was finally dead.

Nimrod was buried in his own city. At the death of Nimrod his kingdom split back into many divisions, and all those parts that Nimrod reigned over were restored to the respective kings of the land. All the people of the house of Nimrod were enslaved to all the other kings of the land for a long time.

Facts taken from:
Genesis 10-11, Jasher 7-27, Josephus *Ant. 1.4.2-3,9* - See also Romans 1

Chapter 22
Israel

אבגדהוזחטיכלמנסעפצקרשת

Hebrew Alphabet

Abraham was the direct descendant of Shem, son of Noah. God promised Abraham that he would be the father of a great nation, through which the Messiah would come and bring salvation to mankind. This promise was also given to

Event	AM
Abraham born	1948
God's promise	2018
Jacob born	2108
Israel goes to Egypt	2238
The Exodus	2448
Babylon exile	3318
Temple destroyed	3338
Israel brought back	3388

Isaac, Abraham's son, and to Jacob, Abraham's grandson. God promised Abraham that his descendants would become enslaved; but at the end of 430 years, He would give them the land of Canaan as an everlasting possession. At the end of the 430 years, *to the day*, Moses led the Exodus from Egypt. Jacob's name was changed to Israel and the country was named after him.

Under Joshua, the new nation of Israel took possession of the land; and under God's direction destroyed the Canaanites. In time Israel adopted some Canaanite paganism, so God caused the nation of Babylon (Iraq) to exile them from their land. God promised that in seventy years they would return. The return came as prophesied.

God then sent the Messiah; but Israel rejected Jesus Christ and allowed Him to be crucified. As prophesied, Israel was dispersed by the Romans. This dispersion lasted 1,816 years. God brought the nation of Israel back from the great

Roman dispersion in AD 1948. This event also took place on the *very day* it was prophesied to occur.

In the last sixty years, 1948-2008 AD, the nation of Israel has seen more than fifty prophecies fulfilled as predicted in the Bible. For a

Event	AD
Temple destroyed	70
Roman exile	132
Israel returns	1948

detailed discussion of these prophecies, see the book, *Ancient Prophecies Revealed.*

Israel will continue to be undefeated and grow in power until the rise of the Antichrist. Seven years after the Antichrist appears on the scene of human history, Jesus Christ will return to earth and set up the Messianic Kingdom, ruling planet Earth from the nation of Israel and its capital city, Jerusalem!

Chapter 23
Kurds

Median Cuneiform

Japheth had a son named Madai, who was originally assigned by lot to the area of Greece, but preferred the area of the Black Sea. So he got permission to resettle into the area around the Black Sea. His descendants became known as the Medes.

> "The sons of Japheth; Gomer, and Magog, and Madai, and Javan, and Tubal, and Meshech, and Tiras." *Genesis 10:2 KJV*

> "And Japheth and his sons went towards the sea and dwelt in the land of their portion, and Madai saw the land of the sea and it did not please him, and he begged a (portion) from Ham and Asshur and Arpachshad, his wife's brother, and he dwelt in the land of Media, near to his wife's brother until this day. And he called his dwelling-place, and the dwelling-place of his sons, Media, after the name of their father Madai." *Jubilees 9:35-36*

In time, the Medes combined with the Persian Empire under Cyrus. The Medes became somewhat absorbed by the peoples around them. Today the Lurs of Iran and the Kurds of Iran, Iraq, and Turkey are their descendants.

Ham's Descendants

African Nations
Canaan
Egypt
Sodom and Gomorrah

Chapter 24
African Nations

Taipothigi ni aina ya kalibu iliyo kule Hegi ina
African Dilect of Swahli

Ham's sons inherited the land to the south, later to be named Africa. Ham's sons were Mizraim, Cush, Phut, and Canaan. His son Mizraim founded Egypt. See the chapter on Egypt's old Kingdom for details. Canaan fathered the Canaanites. See the chapter on Canaan for details. Cush founded Ethiopia, which then included what we call Ethiopia and Sudan, up to the border of Egypt.

One of the sons of Cush, Raamah, had two sons, Sheba and Dedan. These two founded the city states of Sheba and Dedan, located on the coast of Saudi Arabia. Today their descendants are intermingled with the Arabs who live in Saudi Arabia.

The Great Ethiopic War
Phut, along with his sons: Gebul, Hadan, Benah, and Adan, spread out along the Mediterranean coast of Africa. There they established city states and were collectively referred to as the nations of Libya.

Two sons of Mizraim, with their children, the Naphtuhim and the Caphtorim, left Egypt and established cities just inside Libyan territory toward the border of Cush, or Ethiopia. Later, three of the sons of Mizraim, Anom, Lud, and Lehabim, along with their descendants, migrated into Libyan territory along the border of Egypt and the Mediterranean Sea. This sparked what the ancient historians call the Great Ethiopic War.

The Libyans descended and completely wiped out the people and cites of the Naphtuhim and Caphtorim. They then descended upon the Anamim, Ludim, and Lehabim. Pressing further, they were met by the Ethiopians. After many were slaughtered, the Ethiopians pushed the Libyans back and the war finally ended.

In fear of the possibility of another Libyan war, the Pelishtim, descendants of another of Mizraim's sons, began to migrate into the land of Canaan. They became known as the Philistines.

The book of Jasher also records Father Abraham speaking to Anom when he went to Egypt during the three-year famine in Canaan. This places the Great Ethiopic War sometime after 2023 AM. See the chapter on Egypt's Old Kingdom for the complete details on the timeline.

The Herculean War
During the reign of Hercules, the Libyan nations were in disarray. Constant fighting among themselves had even led to anarchy in some of the Libyan tribes. Hercules said he invaded to establish a lasting government, but it was probably more about conquest than government.

Africa received its current name from Aphra, one of Abraham and Keturah's grandsons, who fought in the War under Hercules.

African Freedom under Aeneas
After the Trojan War, Aneas fled the Greeks and found refuge in the Libyan nations. Aneas led a rebellion that ultimately formed the great African Empire. He not only freed Africa from the Greeks and Romans, but became a terror to them as well. See the chapter on Troy for detail on Aeneas and his empire. Aeneas died in the Hebrew year

2411 AM. This was just thirty-seven years before the Exodus from Egypt, during the lifetime of Moses.

Modern Africa

Today the African nations are descendants of these peoples, though very little of the most ancient history remains among them. We are thankful for the records of the Hebrew, Tireians, and Babylonians for what facts we have.

Chapter 25
Canaan

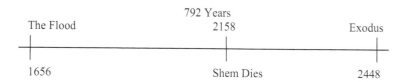

Phoenician Alphabet

The Flood	792 Years 2158	Exodus
1656	Shem Dies	2448

Around one hundred and twenty years after the Flood, God commanded the earth to be divided and the tribes to migrate to their respective places. The sons of Ham, son of Noah, were directed to take the land to the south, later named Africa. One of Ham's sons, Canaan, traveled back up the coast with his family to settle in a land not their own. Today we call this land Israel. Canaan's first-born son, Sidon, (Genesis 10:15) traveled farthest up the coast and founded the city of Sidon. Most archeologists agree that Sidon is one of – if not the – oldest cities in the land.

Tyre
Later, a descendant of Sidon traveled back down the coast to found the city of Tyre. The legendary name for him was Agenor. He is said to have had several children (or descendants) among whom are: Cadmus, Europa, Cilix, and Phoenix. Later the Phoenicians would take their name from Phoenix. The continent of Europe is said to have been named after Europa.

Thebes
In Greek myth, Zeus stole Europa. Cadmus went in search of her. (See the chapter on ancient Greece for more on

135

Zeus and Cilix.) Cadmus traveled to Greece where he founded the city of Thebes. In the legend, he created a seven-sided citadel. Today, archeologists have uncovered the ruins of a seven-sided building in the ancient Greek city of Thebes that bears an inscription with the name of Cadmus.

The historian Herodotus says Cadmus not only built Thebes, but also brought writing to the Greeks. It has long been thought that the most ancient Greek alphabet was created from the ancient Phoenician alphabet.

Abraham, Isaac, and Jacob
Abraham was born in the city of Ur in 1948 AM. In that same year, Nimrod took control and founded what would later be called the Babylonian Empire. Abraham's father, Terah, was a great warrior and became of one Nimrod's generals. Because of a prophecy that a descendant of Abraham would kill Nimrod, Nimrod sought Abraham's life. Terah secretly hid Abraham until he was ten years old. Terah then sent Abraham to live with Noah and Shem and learn about the one true God at Shem's school. Jasher 9:5-6 states Abraham was in Noah's house for thirty-nine years (1958-1997 AM). Abraham returned to Terah's house just four years after the fall of the Tower of Babel. Jasher continues saying not only Abraham, but also his grandson Jacob studied at the school (Jasher 28). For more information on Abraham and Jacob, see the chapter on Ancient Babylon.

Asharah
Asherah was the name of the goddess associated with Baal in the ancient land of Canaan. The name used for her in the LXX shows that she is the same as the goddess Astoreth or Astarte of the Zidonians. She may also be the same as the

Lillith of Isaiah. She is sometimes depicted as having horns and four wings. She is usually seen on coins riding a beast, usually a lion.

As the pantheistic religion started by Nimrod spread into Canaan, the Canaanites added ancestor worship to it. Zidon, Canaan's firstborn son, became the chief deity in the city state of Zidon. In this land he was the "Baal," which means "Lord" in Hebrew. Zidon's wife was the first "Asharah" which means "the princess" in Hebrew. (Ha-Sharah) This form of paganism spread across the land of Canaan, in which each tribe adapted the names of their kings for the same pagan deities.

One of Asharah's symbols was the Asharah pole. This was set up in the high places of Israel, including the Temple, in times of apostasy. In stone reliefs she is sometimes seen with a cone-shaped headdress. The Asharah pole and the headdress are symbols of one of the rituals of her worship. Wiccans will quickly recognize this as the ritual of "drawing down the moon."

In the magic rite of "drawing down the moon," the practitioners draw a circle on the ground and invoke a god or goddess like Hecate, the moon goddess. Then they envision a cone of light coming from the goddess all the way down to them, landing on the edges of their magic circle. Thet believe this energy will then be absorbed by incantation and redirected to a particular use. Not much has changed in 4,000 years.

The Priestesses of Asharah
In Jeremiah 7:18, 44, Israeli women made crescent moon-shaped cakes and dedicated them to Asharah. In this festival she was known as the "Queen of Heaven." We are also told no men could be present at this festival.

Augustine (De civit dei 2.3) says orgies were a part of her worship and some of her priests were eunuchs in women's clothes.

Ezekiel 13:17-21 says the daughters of Israel fastened "magic bands" (kesatot) on their wrists and with them "trapped souls like birds." This word, *kesatot*, occurs only once in the Old Testament. It is related to the Sumerian KI-ShU, meaning a kind of magical imprisonment. It is also related to the Greek word, κιστε, which is a small vial, used in certain mystery rituals of the Dionysian cult. The symbol of the κιστε on Dionysian pictograms is a basket with a snake emerging.

If they actually had vials that were magical (sorcery) that were symbolized by a vemonous serpent and trapped people into doing what they wanted; I believe that Ezekiel was telling us the Asharah priestesses used a very addictive drug to enslave their worshipers. The ingredients of this drug are currently unknown. Revelation 9:21 says one of the major sins in the last days will be sorcery, or drug use.

Information from:
The Targums of Onkelos and Jonathan Ben Uzziel Jasher, Josephus, Jewish Encyclopedia, and the Ante-Nicene Fathers

Canaanites Helped Build Nimrod's Tower

Chapter 26
Egypt's Old Kingdom

Egyptian Hieroglyphics

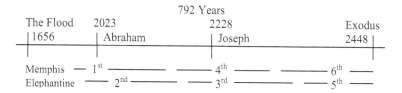

As we learned in chapter 2, the Flood occurred 1,656 years after Creation and the Exodus from Egypt occurred 2,448 years after Creation. This proves there were 792 years between the Flood and the Exodus.

We shall see that ancient Egyptian records total about one hundred years less from Menes founding the nation of Egypt to Egypt's destruction. Assuming it took about one hundred years for each of Noah's sons to have enough children and grandchildren to spread out and create cities and eventually nations, this works out just right.

There are several sources for the Dynasties of Egypt's Old Kingdom. Among these are:

1. Temple of Seti in Abydos, Egypt
2. The Turin Papyri
3. Egyptian historian Manetho

When we compare these to Jewish sources like the Biblical book of Genesis, the Book of Jasher, the Seder Olam, the Talmud, the Mishna, the Codex Judaica, and others, we can map these out with great detail.

The temple of Seti, was created by Pharoah Seti of the twenty-third Dynasty. The records of the first nineteen dynasties are carved on its walls in Egyptian hieroglyphics.

Although the names used for each pharaoh vary by dialect when comparing the Turin papyri, Manetho, and Seti's temple, the dates given for each pharaoh's reign are almost identical in each of the three sources.

The Old Kingdom

The earliest records of Egypt show six dynasties that comprise what is called the Old Kingdom. Some event happened at the end of the Old Kingdom that obliterated all of Egypt. Secular historians still debate what this might have been.

As Christians, we know from the book of Exodus that Egypt was destroyed by the ten plagues that God sent through Moses.

The Egyptian army was destroyed in the Red Sea. The cattle, food supply, and the firstborn of all Egyptian people and animals were destroyed by the plagues. In addition, Israelite slave labor left Egypt with a large portion of the nation's wealth. The events described in the biblical account of the Exodus would destroy any empire.

Memphis and Elephantine

Menes (Mizriam) is credited with founding Memphis, the capital of the First Dynasty. Its ruins lie twelve miles south of modern Cairo. Memphis served as the capital of the First, Fourth, and Sixth dynasties. Elephantine is an island in the Nile River, on the border of Egypt and Nubia. Elephantine was the capital of the Second, Third, and Fifth dynasties.

Egyptologists have long assumed that the Six dynasties ruled one after the other, in six consecutive periods. In reality, there were always two dynasties ruling *at the same time*. The First and Second were contemporary, and so were the Third with Fourth and the Fifth with the Sixth.

We will see that the First, Fourth, and Sixth dynasties were consecutive and ruled from Memphis. The Second, Third, and Fifth dynasties were consecutive and ruled from Elephantine.

The following chart is created from the three Egyptian sources and shows the First and Second Dynasties of Egypt's Old Kingdom. According to these texts, Menes (Mizraim) founded Egypt and began the First Dynasty. Menes was said to be a great explorer and his life was cut short when he was killed by a hippo. As we will see in the chapter on Egypt and Abraham, an Assyrian migrated to Egypt and began the Second Dynasty. The Hebrews called his name Rikayn, but the Egyptians called him Boethos. He was the first to be called Pharaoh.

First and Second Dynasties

Date	Dynasty I 253 years	Dynasty II 302 years
	1 Menes (Mizraim) (52)	
	2 Athothisis (Anom) (57)	
	3 Kenkenes (31)	
~2000	4 Uenephes (Oswiris) (23)	1 Boethos (Rikayn) (38)
	5 Usaphais (20)	2 Kaiechos (39)
	6 Miebis (26)	3 Binothris (47)
	7 Semempses (18)	4 Tlas (17)
	8 Bieneches (26)	5 Sethenes 41)
		6 Chaires (17)
		7 Nephercheres (25)
	Great famine	8 Sesochris (48)
		9 Cheneres (30)

Years of reign are in parenthesis.

Athothisis was remembered as a great physician. Kaiechos is remembered as the one who began the worship of Apis bulls and Macedonian goats as gods.

There was a great famine during the reign of Uenephes. As we will see in the chapter on Egypt and Abraham, this was the famine that caused Abraham to migrate to Egypt for three years.

Third and Fourth Dynasties
Djoser was the Pharaoh of Joseph's time. Manetho tells us that the seven-year famine occurred in the eighteenth year of the reign of Djoser Teti.

Dynasty III	Dynasty IV
214 years	**274 years**
1 Nebka, Necherophes (28)	1 Soris (29)
2 Djoser, Tosorthos (29) *Joseph's time*	2 Suphis (53)
3 Tyresis (7)	3 Cheops (66)
4 Mesochris (17)	4 Mencheres (63)
5 Setes, Suphis (16)	5 Ratoeses (25)
6 Djoser Teti, Tosertasis (19)	6 Bicheres (22)
7 Ahtes, Aches (42)	7 Sebercheres (7)
8 Nebkara, Sephuris (30)	8 Thamphthis (9)
9 Neferkara, Kerpheres (26)	

Years of reign are in parenthesis.

Fifth and Sixth Dynasties

Pepy II was the Pharaoh that persecuted the Children of Israel. The empire of his son, Neferkare the younger, was destroyed by Moses.

Dynasty V	Dynasty VI
108 years	**172 years**
1 Usercheres*, Userkaf (28)	1 Teti, Othoes (30)
2 Sephres, Sahure (13)	2 Meryre Pepi I, Phios (49)
3 Nephercheres, Neferirkare Kakai (20)	3 Menrenre Antiemsaf I Methesuphis (14)*
4 Siseres, Shepseskare Isi (7)*	4 Neferkare Pepi II (94) Phiops II
5 Cheres, Neferefre (7)*	5 Menthesuphis (1) Merenre Antiemsaf II
6 Rathures, Neuserre (3)*	6 Netjerykare (0)
7 Mencheres, Menkauhor Akauhor (8)	
8 Tancheres, Djedkare Isesi (39)	
9 Onnus, Unis (30)	

Years of reign are in parenthesis. *Co-rule

Based on Manetho's records as corrected by Jasher, the following chart shows the total time (in parenthesis) of each dynasty and total time dynasties were ruling from Memphis and Elephantine.

Memphis (699)	Elephantine (624)
First – (253)	Second – (302)
Fourth – (274)	Third – 2120-2334 AM (214)
Sixth – 2278-2448 AM (172)	Fifth – 2340-2448 AM (108)

The Sixth Dynasty tried to hold on for almost two years after the Exodus. The Fifth Dynasty remained intact for almost twenty-four years after the Exodus, as a vassel state, before its final fall.

Now let us proceed to verifiy who was ruling Upper and Lower Egypt when Abraham went there during the three-year famine.

Chapter 27
Egypt and Abraham

Egyptian Hieroglyphics

		792 Years	
The Flood	2023	2228	Exodus
1656	Abraham	Joseph	2448

Memphis — 1st ————— ————— 4th ——— ————— 6th ———
Elephantine ——— 2nd ————— ——— 3rd ————— ——— 5th ———

With proof of Egypt's Old Kingdom existing less than 700 years, we now turn to the books of Genesis and Jasher for Hebrew historical dates.

Mizraim
Genesis 10:6 details Mizraim, the son of Ham, founded the nation of Egypt. This would make him the first king of the First Dynasty of Egypt's Old Kingdom, called Menes in the Egyptian records. Both Genesis 10:13 and Jasher 7:11 record Mizraim's son, Anom, succeeded the throne. Jasher 14:2 records that Anom's son, Oswiris, became the third king of the First Dynasty. In time, Anom would be deified and worshiped as the Egyptian god Amon-Ra, and Oswiris, as the god Osiris.

Ancient Egyptian Records
The Egyptian records mentioned in the chapter on Egypt's Old Kingdom state Menes (Mizraim) founded the nation of Egypt and built the city of Memphis. Mizraim was killed by a hippopotamus during an expedition further into Africa. In the time of Uenephes, a great famine occurred. This corresponds to an event in the reign of Boethos, when a great chasm opened up at Bubastis and many perished.

This gives us some possible insight into the cause of the great famine.

In the ancient Indian list, Boethis, the first ruler of the Second Dynasty, is called Riteyu or Riceyu. This gives more proof to the Jewish history given by the book of Jasher.

First and Second Dynasties

Date	Dynasty I 253 years	Dynasty II 302 years
	1 Menes (Mizraim) (52)	
	2 Athothisis (Anom) (57)	
	3 Kenkenes (31)	
~2000	4 Uenephes (Oswiris) (23)	1 Boethos (Rikayn) (38)
	5 Usaphais (20)	2 Kaiechos (39)
	6 Miebis (26)	3 Binothris (47)
	7 Semempses (18)	4 Tlas (17)
	8 Bieneches (26)	5 Sethenes 41)
		6 Chaires (17)
		7 Nephercheres (25)
		8 Sesochris (48)
		9 Cheneres (30)

Years of reign are in parenthesis.

Abraham's Three-year Famine

Genesis 12 records Abraham moved to Canaan when he was seventy-five years old. Shortly after the move, there was a severe famine in Canaan. So Abraham went down to Egypt until the famine was over. Looking at Jasher 13.22, 13.5, and 16.22, we have a clear record of Abraham settling in Canaan and the three-year famine occurring during the years of 2023-2026 AM.

This famine was only 367 years after the Flood and thirty years after the fall of the Tower of Babel. As we learned in the chapter on Babylon, Jasher 15 and 16 records that Nimrod was a contemporary of both Oswiris and Abraham. Nimrod was the fourth generation from Noah, and Oswiris was fifth, while Abraham was the tenth generation from Noah.

As noted previously, the first few generations lived into their 400's. We are told when Abraham stayed in Egypt for three years, during the famine of 2023-2026 AM, he met both King Oswiris and Pharaoh Rikayn. (Jasher 15) King Oswiris was still ruling due to his incredibly long lifespan, being the great-grandson of Ham.

Where did the word "Pharaoh" come from?
In Jasher 14 there is a man named Rikayn, who came from the land of Shinar to Egypt to seek his fortune.

Rikayn came up with a plan. He hired a group of men with superior weapons from his native country and took control of the sacred burial places in Egypt. He ordered that no one be allowed to bury their dead unless they paid him two hundred pieces of silver. This made him rich. Rikayn sent many presents of gold and jewels to Oswiris, king of Egypt, to win his favor before the cries of the people reached him. In time he cunningly usurped control of all of Egypt.

Rikayn and all kings after him were called "Pharaoh" meaning, "Lord of the dead," or more literally "he who causes the dead to pay taxes." Rikayn became the first Pharaoh of the Second Dynasty and began ruling from Elephantine.

Note: Josephus says that astronomy was unknown in Egypt until Abraham brought it there from Chaldea. It is

149

also possible that Rikayn brought it to Egypt, rather than Abraham.

We can conclude that Uenephes (Oswiris) of the First Dynasty and Boethos (Rikayn) of the Second Dynasty were ruling when Abraham came to Egypt in the Hebrew year 2023 AM.

It is possible that Ham may have still been alive when Abraham visited Egypt.

Ham

Ham settled in Africa with his sons. Mizriam founded Egypt and Cush founded Nubia, which at one time extended from the border of Egypt all the way to Ethiopia. It is logical to look for Ham in the midst of his children. The city of Elephantine, which became the capital of the southern dynasties, was right on the border of Egypt and Nubia. Secular historians tell us that in the Third Dynasty Elephantine was called Abu. The chief god worshiped in Elephantine was Chnum, the ram-headed god. Egyptians said he was the original creator of the other Egyptian gods including Menes (Mizriam), who founded the first Egyptian Daynasty.

Chnum would be Ham, deified and worshiped. Notice that the name Chnum is very close to the Hebrew name for Ham: Cham. He is also said to have created a series of tunnels under the city. It is very possible that Ham is buried in one of those tunnels. This may have led to the Greek myth of Theseus and the Minotaur. The Minotaur was a bull-headed man instead of a ram-headed one.

Now let's look at the Egyptian and Hebrew records that give us information about the time that Joseph would have been ruling in Egypt.

Note:

Josephus says (Ant.1.8) the Egyptians worshiped false gods in Abraham's time. Manetho says the second pharaoh of the Second Dynasty, Kaiechos, was the first to introduce the worship of bulls and goats into Egypt. So the first and second kings of the Second Dynasty had to have ruled prior to (or were co-ruling at the time of) the famine of Abraham.

If Rikayn was the first ruler of the Second Dynasty, then the Second Dynasty started at the time of Abraham. That means it could only last about one hundred years to fit into Jasher's timetable, instead of 302 years as Manetho records.

If Rikayn was only the first to be called Pharaoh, and he usurped the Elephantine throne, then Manetho could be correct in his estimate of a 302-year reign for the Second Dynasty. Actually, one hundred and three years back from the beginning of the next dynasty would put us into the time of Abraham and the first year of the reign of Pharaoh Nephercheres of the Second Dynasty.

Chapter 28
Egypt and Joseph

Egyptian Hieroglyphics

		792 Years	
The Flood	2023	2228	Exodus
1656	Abraham	Joseph	2448

Memphis — 1st ——— ——— 4th ——— ——— 6th ——
Elephantine —— 2nd ——— —— 3rd ——— —— 5th ——

We learned from the chapter on basic chronology that Joseph started reigning in the Hebrew year 2228 AM. The book of Jasher, along with the Talmud, gives us the date of 2235-2341 AM for the seven-year famine.

Ancient Egyptian Records
When we look at the Egyptian records mentioned in the chapter on Egypt's Old Kingdom for the pharaohs that would have been ruling close to the date of 2228 AM, we find Pharaoh Dojer of the Third Dynasty and Pharaoh Bicheres of the Fourth Dynasty.

Joseph
In 2228 AM, Joseph interpreted Pharaoh's dream of seven years of plenty and seven years of famine. This same year Joseph became Viceroy of Egypt. We are told in Genesis 41:45 that Pharaoh renamed Joseph "Zaphnath-Paaneah."

Manetho records a seven-year famine occurred in the eighteenth year of the reign of Djoser. If this seven-year famine is the same as the one Joseph predicted, then the eighteenth year of Djoser was 2235 AM.

Third and Fourth Dynasties

Dynasty III 214 years	Dynasty IV 274 years
1 Nebka, Necherophes (28)	1 Soris (29)
2 Djoser, Tosorthos (29)	2 Suphis (53)
3 Tyresis (7)	3 Cheops (66)
4 Mesochris (17)	4 Mencheres (63)
5 Setes, Suphis (16)	5 Ratoeses (25)
6 Djoser Teti, Tosertasis (19)	6 Bicheres (22)
7 Ahtes, Aches (42)	7 Sebercheres (7)
8 Nebkara, Sephuris (30)	8 Thamphthis (9)
9 Neferkara, Kerpheres (26)	

Years of reign are in parenthesis.

The Viceroy of Djoser, Imhotep, designed the step pyramid at Sakkara. On a rock monument at Sehel, there is an inscription telling how Pharaoh consulted the wise Imhotep about a seven-year famine. In another inscription near the step pyramid, the builder is referred to as Zanakht – very close to Joseph's Egyptian name Zaphnath-Paaneah as given in Genesis.

Imhotep's Legacy

Both Imhotep and Joseph lived to be one hundred and ten years old. When Imhotep was one hundred years old, his wisdom was tested by new court officials by asking him to create an oasis in the desert. He engineered a feeder canal from the Nile to his man-made lake. Today in the region of El-Fayoum, southwest of Cairo, there still remains the man-made fresh water lake called Birqet Qarun. It is fed by a canal stretching from the Nile to the Basin. The canal is known as Bahr Yousef or the Sea of Joseph! Since this was built during the last ten years of Joseph's life, we can date Birqet Qarun's construction between 2299-2309 AM.

Conclusion

We can conclude that Joseph, also known as Imhotep, rose to power in the Hebrew year 2228 AM. The seven-year famine lasted from 2235 to 2241 AM and that these were the eighteenth though the twenty-fourth years of the reign of Pharaoh Djoser of the Third Dynasty of Egypt's Old Kingdom!

Chapter 29
Egypt and the Exodus

Egyptian Hieroglyphics

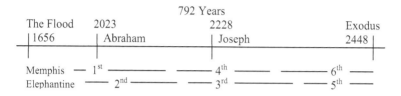

		792 Years		
The Flood	2023	2228		Exodus
1656	Abraham	Joseph		2448

Memphis — 1st		4th		6th
Elephantine — 2nd		3rd		5th

Using the Egyptian and Hebrew history texts cited in the chapter on Egypt's Old Kingdom, we can piece together the following story:

Pepi II and Neferkare (Shorty)
Jasher places the Exodus at 2448 AM. The Pharaoh of the Exodus, Adikam, ruled four years, including three years co-ruling with his sick father. Adikam was a dwarf; so, the Hebrews called him Adikam Ahuz. Ahuz means "short" in Hebrew. Adikam's father was Pharaoh Melol. During the last ten years of his life, Melol had leprosy but still ruled a total of ninety-four years. Melol reigned from 2353 to 2447 AM. Joseph reigned from 2228 to 2309 AM. Thus Melol would be the "Pharaoh who knew not Joseph." Melol was the pharaoh who started the heavy persecution of the Israelites.

The Egyptian records in the Temple of Abydos, the Turin papyrus, and the Egyptian historian Manetho, show that Pharaoh Neferkare Pepi II (also called Phiops II and NetjerKhau) was the longest living Pharaoh in the Old Kingdom. He became Pharaoh at the age of six and lived

155

until he was one hundred years old. His son, Neferkare the Younger, (also called Menthesuphis and Merenre Antiemsaf II) ruled only one year after his father's death. This exactly matches the description Jasher gives.

The last ruler listed in the texts is Nitokerti, the wife of Neferkare, the Younger. The Hebrews called her Gedudah. With her husband gone and her firstborn son, Netjerykare, killed in the last great plague, she alone was left to rule. In this male-dominated society, a queen would be allowed to rule only when there were no male heirs.

Menrenre Antiemsaf I ruled fourteen years. This was three years with Pepy I and eleven years with Pepy II, when he grew from six to seventeen years of age. Moses was born in 2368 AM (See Jasher 66). So, the Sixth Dynasty lasted a total of 174 years plus the two years Nitokerti ruled after the Exodus.

Jasher		Manetho
174 years		**Sixth dynasty**
		Teti, Othoes (30)
2304-2353		Meryre Pepi I, Phios (49)
2350-2364	Co-Rule	Menrenre Antiemsaf I (14)
2353- 2447	Melol (94)	Neferkare Pepi II (94)
2447-2448	Adikam (1)	Neferkare the Younger (1)
		3 year co-rule; 1 yr sole rule
		Netjerykare (0)
2448	**Exodus**	
2448-2450	Gedudah	Nitokerti (2)

Years of reign are in parenthesis. Dates are given in AM.

Photo from Wikipedia

This famous Egyptian statue of a dwarf contains the inscription stating this dwarf was Seneb, a servant of Pepi II of the Sixth Dynasty. We now know from the book of Jasher, this "servant" was actually his second-born son and the pharaoh of the Exodus.

King Kikianus

Jasher 76 and Josephus Ant. 2.10 describe Moses leading an army against the Ethiopians at Elephantine under King Kikianus. The same year that Moses fled Memphis, King Kikianus defeated the uprising of Aram and the Kedemites. Upon his return, Kikianus discovered that the city of Elephantine had been taken over by Balaam and his sons. Kikianus besieged the city for nine years. He then died of a disease in 2395 AM. Moses delivered the city and ruled

157

it for thirty-nine years. The city was then turned over to Menacrus, the son of King Kikianus in 2434 AM.

Here is a cross referenced chart comparing Manetho's Egyptian king list with Jasher's. Notice the Egyptian texts have the reigns of Moses and Menacrus switched, but the years are accurate. The reigns of the usurpers are the same years as King Kikianus. Onnus managed to hold on as a vassal state for twenty-four years after the Exodus.

Jasher		Manetho
216 years		**Third Dynasty**
2120-2148		Nebka, Necherophes (28)
2148-2177		Djoser Tosorthos (29)
2177-2184		Tyresis (7)
2184-2201		Mesochris (17)
2201-2217		Setes, Suphis (16)
2217-2236		Djoser Teti (19)
2228	Joseph begans Reign	
2235-2242	7 yr Famine	
2236-2270		Aches (42)
2270-2310	Magron (40)	Nebkara (30)
	Joseph dies 2309	
2310-2336		Neferkara (26)
108 years		**Fifth Dynasty**
2340-2368		Usercheres*, Userkaf (28)
2362-2375		Sephres, Sahure (13)
2375-2395	Kikianus (20) ➡	Neferirkare Kakai (20)
	Balaam and sons (During Kakianus reign.)	Siseres (7) Cheres (7 or 20) Rathures (1 or 3)
2395-2434	Moses (39)	Djedkare Isesi (39)
2434-2442	Menacrus ⬅	Mencheres (8)
2442-2472		Onnus (30)
2448	**Exodus**	

Years of reign are in parenthesis. Dates are given in AM.
* 6 year co-rule

For a detailed analysis of the Exodus, beginning in 2448 AM, see the chapter on basic chronology.

Moses' first eighty years
In Acts 7:23-30, Stephen said that Moses lived forty years in Egypt and forty years in the wilderness. The Exodus occurred when he was eighty years old.

Jasher shows Moses was eighteen when he left Egypt. He lived ten years in Kikianus' camp, spent thirty-nine years as the king of Cush (ruling from Elephantine), then lived thirteen years in Midian, until he led the Exodus at the age of eighty.

This may seem like a contradiction, but it's not. Stephen gave the history from the viewpoint of the Memphis-ruled Sixth Dynasty, while Jasher and Josephus give the events as counted from the Elephantine-ruled Fifth Dynasty.

When Moses killed the Egyptian and fled at age eighteen and became a part of Kikianus' camp, Cush was controlled by Egypt from Memphis. When Moses became strong enough, the southern Fifth Dynasty kingdom seceded from Egypt.

So from the point of view of Memphis, Moses spent forty years under their control and forty years in the wilderness outside their control. However, from the point of view of Elephantine, Moses spent eighteen years with Egypt and ten in their army, thirty-nine years as their king, and thirteen years in the wilderness.

Other Proofs
Other proofs supporting the Exodus from Egypt occurred at the end of the Sixth Dynasty, or Old Kingdom are:

Black Granite Naos at Ismailia

Originally found in the City of El Arish, this Naos stone is now housed in a museum in Ismailia, Egypt. It contains an inscription written in Egyptian hieroglyphics, stating Pharaoh's entire army was destroyed in some kind of "whirlpool." This is proof, written in stone, of the destruction of the Egyptian army in the Red Sea as recorded in Genesis.

The Leiden Papyrus

The Leiden Papyrus, also called the Ippuwer Papyrus or "The admonitions of an Egyptian sage," is an account of the plagues that destroyed the Sixth Dynasty. Immanuel Velikowsky, in his book *Ages in Chaos*, p. 26-28 gave a detailed account of the Leiden Papyrus. Here are a few quotes from the papyrus describing the same plagues recorded in the book of Exodus.

Water to Blood

2:5-6 Plague is everywhere. Blood is everywhere.

7:4 He who poured water on the ground; he has captured the stong man in his misery.

2:10 The river is blood. Men shrink from tasting... and thirst for water.

Plague Hail and Fire

2:10 Gates, columns and walls are consumed by fire.

Plague of Insects

6:1-4 No fruit or herbs are found... Grain has perished on every side.

Plague of Darkness

9:2-3 The land is not light...

9:8 -10 Destruction... the land is in darkness.

Plague of Death of the Firstborn

2:13 Men are few. He who places his brother in the ground is everywhere.

4:3 The offspring of nobility are laid out on the high ground.

The Spoiling of Egypt

3:3 Gold, bluestone, silver, malichate, carnelian, bronze... are fastened to the necks of female slaves.

The Pillar of Fire

7:1 Behold the fire mounted up on high. Its burning goes forth before the enemies of the land.

Conclusion

We have ample proof in Egyptian records to show the people, events, and dates of the Biblical record are completely true.

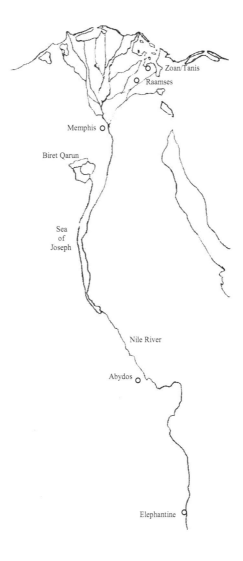

Zoan/Tanis

Raamses

Memphis

Biret Qarun

Sea
of
Joseph

Nile River

Abydos

Elephantine

Chapter 30
Sodom and Gomorrah

𐤄𐤅𐤓𐤌𐤂𐤅𐤃𐤁𐤇𐤔𐤓𐤅𐤌𐤃𐤅𐤎

South West Semitic Script

Zoar and the Dead Sea

In 1998 AM Bela founded the city of Zoar. This happened the second year after the fall of the Tower of Babel. Bela was an Assyrian who left Assyria and came to Canaan. This is in the territory Noah gave to Shem, Bela's forefather, and founded his town there. So he had every right to settle there. Bela left his homeland because of Nimrod's evil government. The city of Zoar stayed away from paganism. The cities of Sodom and Gomorrah were founded by Canaanites and in time they adopted paganism to such an extreme measure God destroyed them with fire. This is why Lot went to Zoar, and the city of Zoar was spared. As the area filled up with water, forming the Dead Sea, the city of Zoar or Bela may have been abandoned.

The book of Jasher contains over five pages of information dealing with the customs, paganism, and government structure of Sodom and Gomorrah.

Sodom and Elam

In 1996 AM, 340 years after the Flood, there was a war between the sons of Ham and Chedorlaomer, the ruler of Elam. Sodom, Gomorrah, and the other cities of the plains were conquered in the year 1997 AM and forced to pay tribute to Chedorlaomer for almost twelve years. In 2008 AM, 352 years after the Flood, the five cities rebelled.

In the Year 2034 AM Chedorlaomer crushed the rebellion and recaptured Sodom and Gomorrah, but in this battle

Abraham's nephew, Lot, was also captured. This caused Abraham to enter the war. He destroyed the Elamite forces, killing Chedorlaomer and freeing Lot, along with Sodom and Gomorrah.

The Destruction of Sodom

Over time, the cities of Sodom and Gomorrah became exceedingly wicked. The people of Sodom and Gomorrah observed the four seasonal pagan holidays with dances timbrels, and orgies. Their courts became unjust, allowing the wicked free reign. Homosexuality was rampant.

The inhabitants became more and more wicked until in 2047 AM, just 391 years after the Flood, the LORD destroyed the cities of Sodom and Gomorrah by raining down fire on them. This destroyed the whole area, which eventually filled up with water. Today this area is called the Dead Sea.

Sodom and Gomorrah existed before Zoar was settled, so the cities of the plain existed over fifty years. Notice it takes less than fifty years for a group of people to become utterly corrupt!

Information taken from the books of Jasher and Josephus.

Chapter 31
Remaining Nations

These remaining nations have barely a trace of information linking them to the Flood.

African Nations
Other than Egypt and Libya, all we know of the other African nations is they should all be traced back to Ham, son of Noah.

England
In ancient times England was called Tarshish by the Hebrews. There are prophecies in Scripture about Tarshish that were fulfilled by England.

Hungary
The Hungarian Chronicle states the Hungarians were descended from the Scythians. The Scythians (southern Russians) were descended from Magog. See the chapter on Russia.

Korea
A legend among the people of Korea states they are descended from Yocktan, son of Eber, son of Selah, son of Arphaxad, son of Shem, son of Noah.

Libya
Originally the name Libya referred to all the northern coastline of Africa. Today the name remains the name of a country in northern Africa.

Mongolia
Mongolia was founded by Ongolis son of Meshech, son of Japheth, son of Noah. See chapter on Russia for full details.

Turkey
Turkey should be descended partly from the sons of Togarmah and other peoples. The house of Togarmah seems to be Georgia, Armenia, and part of Turkey.

USA
The United States is populated by peoples from all over the globe. If it were mentioned in prophecy, it would be referred to as being born out of Tarshish, or England.

Yemen
Yemen is called Teman in ancient Hebrew. The Yemanites are Arabs and thus descended from the sons of Abraham. They are also said to be descended from some of the sons of Ham. Legend has it that Shem laid the foundation for the city of Sanaa, anciently called "Madinat Sam." If so, this would be one of the oldest post-Flood cities on Earth.

Damascus, Syria
Josephus states in his *Antiquites 1.6.4*, Damascus, Syria, was founded by Uz, grandson of Shem and ancestor of Abraham. Damascus is one of the oldest cities in the Middle East.

Appendices

Appendix A
Timeline Charts

Births and Deaths

0001-0930	Adam (930)	2108-2255	Jacob (147)
0130-1042	Seth (912)	2108-2255	Esau (147)
0235-1140	Enos (905)	2164-2214	Leah (50)
0325-1235	Cainan (910)	2164-2209	Rachel (45)
0395-1290	Mahalaleel (895)	2188-????	Reuel (Esau 80)
0460-1422	Jared (962)	2193-2317	Reuben (124)
0622-987	Enoch* (365)	2193-2313	Simeon (120)
0687-1656	Methuselah (969)	2194-2331	Levi (137)
0874-1651	Lamech (777)	2195-2324	Judah (129)
0974-????	Namaah	2196-2310	Zebulon (114)
1056-2006	Noah (950)	2196-2321	Gad (125)
1556-????	Japheth	2197-2319	Issachar (122)
1558-2158	Shem (600)	2197-2320	Asher (123)
1656	Flood	2198-2318	Dan (120)
1658-2096	Arphaxad (438)	2199-2309	Joseph (110)
1693-2126	Shelah (433)	???? -2208	Laban ()
1723-2187	Eber (464)	2209-2318	Benjamin (109)
1757-1996	Peleg (239)	2216-2349	Kohath (133)
1787-2026	Reu (239)	2225-????	Perez and Zerah
1819-2048	Serug (205)	2233-????	Ephraim, Manasseh
1849-1997	Nahor I (148)	2298-2488	Balaam (190)
1878-2083	Terah (205)	2338-2379	Jochebed (141) Levi
1908-2123	Nimrod (215)	2364-2488	Miriam (124)
1948-2123	Abraham (175)	2365-2488	Aaron (123)
1958-2085	Sarah (127)	2368-2488	Moses (120)
1947-2087	Lot (140)	2406-2516	Joshua (110)
2034-2172	Ishmael (138)	2445-????	Gershom (Moses)
2048-2228	Isaac (180)	2446-????	Eliezer (Moses)
2075-2208	Rebekah (133)		

* Enoch did not die but was translated or raptured.

Marriages

1056 Lemech (182) married Ashuma

1554 Noah (498) married Namaah

1651 Shem, Ham, and Japheth married the daughters of Eliakim

1998 Abraham (50) married Sarah (40)

2088 Isaac (40) married Rebekah (13)

2088 Abraham (140) married Keturah

2193 Jacob (85) married Leah and Rachel (29)

2216 Levi (22) married Adia

2445 Moses (77) married Zipporah

1 Adam created by God

130 Seth born of Adam (130)

235 Enos born of Seth (105)

325 Cainan born of Enos (90)

365 Cainan (40) becomes king.

395 Mahalaleel born of Cainan (70)

460 Jared born of Mahalaleel (65)

622 Enoch born of Jared (162)

687 Methuselah born of Enoch (65)

687 Enoch (65) becomes king.

874 Lamech born of Methuselah (187)

930 Adam died (930)

930 Methuselah (243) becomes king

974 Naamah born of Enoch (352)

987 Enoch (365) translated by God.

1042 Seth died (912)

1056 Lemech (182) married Ashuma

1056 Noah born of Lamech (182) on Rosh HaShanah

1140 Enos died (905)

1235 Cainan died (910)

1290 Mahalaleel died (895)

1422 Jared died (962)

1554 Noah (498) married Naamah

1556 Japheth born of Noah (500) and Naamah (582)

Ancient Post-Flood History

1558 Shem born of Noah (502) and Naamah (584)
1651 Lamech died (777)
1651 Noah (595) commanded to build the Ark.
1651 Shem, Ham, and Japheth marry the daughters of Eliakim
1656 Methuselah died (969)
1656 The Flood
1657 Noahide covenant and laws established
1658 Arphaxad born of Shem (100)
1693 Selah born of Arphaxad (35)
1723 Eber born of Selah (30)
1757 Peleg born of Eber (34)
1787 Reu born of Peleg (30)
1819 Serug born of Reu (32)
1849 Nahor I born of Serug (30)
1878 Terah born of Nahor I (29)
1908 Nimrod born of Cush
1948 Nimrod (40) began his reign.
1948 Abram born of Terah (70)
1958 Sarai born of Nahor II
1958 Abram (10) went to live with Noah (902)
1987 Lot born of Nahor II
1993 The Tower of Babel fell.
1996 Peleg died (239)
1996 Chedorlaomer of Elam conquered Sodom and Gomorrah
1997 Nahor I died (148)
1997 Abram (49) went to Ur of the Chaldeans
1998 Abram (50) married Sarai (40)
2000 Abram (52) fled from Nimrod to Noah (944)
2003 Abram (55) went to Canaan
2006 Noah died (950)
2008 Sodom and Gomorrah rebeled against Chedoraomer
2013 Nimrod (105) went to war with Chedorlaomer
2018 Abram (70) went to Terah (140) in Hebron
          (the 430 years began; Gal. 3:16,17)
2023 Abraham (75) and Lot (36) went to Caanan
2023 Rikayn becomes Pharaoh
2026 Reu died (239)
2034 Ishmael born of Abraham (86)
2047 God commanded Abraham (99) to practice circumcision.
2048 Sodom and Gomorrah destroyed
2048 Isaac born of Abraham (100) and Sarah (90)
2048 Serug died (205)

2075 Rebekah born of Bethuel
2083 Terah died (205)
2085 Isaac (37) offered
2085 Sarah died (127)
2088 Isaac (40) married Rebekah (13)
2088 Abraham (140) married Keturah
2096 Arphaxad died (438)
2108 Esau and Jacob born of Isaac (60) and Rebekah (33)
2123 Abraham died (175)
2123 Nimrod killed (215) by Esau (15)
2123 Esau (15) sold his birthright to Jacob (15)
2126 Selah died (433)
2126 Jacob (18) went to live with Shem (568)
2158 Shem died at 600
2158 Jacob (50) left Shem and went to live with Isaac (110)
2164 Leah and Rachel born of Laban
2171 Jacob (63) fled to Eber (448)
2172 Ishmael died (138)
2185 Jacob (77) went to Isaac (137) in Hebron
2185 Jacob (77) went to Laban in Padan-Aram
2187 Eber died (464)
2188 Reuel born of Esau (80)
2193 Jacob (85) married Leah (29) and Rachel (29)
2193 Reuben born of Jacob (85) and Leah (29)
2193 Simeon born of Jacob (85) and Leah (29)
2194 Levi born of Jacob (86) and Leah (30)
2195 Judah born of Jacob (87) and Leah (31)
2196 Zebulun born of Jacob (88) and Leah (32)
2196 Gad born of Jacob (88)
2197 Issachar born of Jacob (89) and Leah (33)
2197 Asher born of Jacob (89)
2198 Dan born of Jacob (90)
2199 Joseph born of Jacob (91) and Rachel (35)
2206 Jacob (98) returned to Isaac (158)
2207 Jacob (99) went to Bethel
2208 Rebekah died (133)
2208 Laban died
2209 Rachel died (45) birthing Benjamin of Israel (Jacob) (101)
2214 Leah died (50)
2216 Joseph (17) sold into Egypt
2216 Levi (22) married Adia (daughter of Joktan son of Eber)
2216 Kohath born of Levi (22)
2216 Joseph (17) imprisoned

2225 Perez and Zerah born of Judah (30)
2226 Joseph (27) interprets two dreams
2228 Isaac died (180)
2228 Joseph (29 or 30) began his reign in Egypt
2233 Manasseh born of Joseph (34)
2233 Ephriam born of Joseph (34)
2238 Israel (130) went to Egypt
2238 Jochebed born of Levi (44) on the way to Egypt
2255 Israel died (147)
2255 Esau died (147)
2270 Magron became Pharaoh
2298 Baalam born of Beor
2309 Joseph died (110)
2310 Zebulun died (114)
2313 Simeon died (120)
2317 Reuben died (124)
2318 Dan died (120)
2319 Issachar died (122)
2320 Asher died (123)
2321 Gad died (125)
2324 Judah died (129)
2331 Levi died (137)
2332 Egyptian slavery began
2353 Melol became Pharaoh
2364 Miriam born of Amram and Jochebed (126)
2365 Aaron born of Amram and Jochebed (127)
2368 Moses born of Amram and Jochebed (130)
2406 Joshua born of Nun
2445 Moses (77) married Zipporah
2447 Moses saw the burning bush
2447 The miracle of Moses' staff turned into a serpent
2448 The plagues against Egypt
2448 The Exodus from Egypt (fifteenth of the first month)
2448 The Ten Commandments given by God (sixth of the third month); (the 430 years end, Gal. 3:16,17)
2448 Manna sent from Heaven (fifteenth of the second month)
2448 The Tabernacle built (five months)
2448 Aaron (83) anointed High Priest 23rd of the 12th month
2449 The Tabernacle dedicated (first of the first month)
2449 Passover first observed (thirteenth of the first month)
2449 The cloud left the Tabernacle (twentith of the first month)
2488 Israelites returned to Canaan (first of the first month)

2488 Miriam died (124)
2488 Aaron died (123) on Mt. Hor (first of the fifth month)
2488 Baalam died (190) in Moab
2488 Moses died (120) on Mt. Nebo
2489 Joshua (82) crossed the Jordan (tenth of the first month)
2489 First Passover in Canaan (fourteenth of the first month; Manna ceases)
2489 Joshua (82) instructed by God about Jericho
2494 The land of Canaan conquered by the Israelites
2503 Land of Israel divided among the 12 tribes
2514 Joshua (108) blessed the Israelites
2516 Joshua died (110)
     17 yr rule of elders
2533 1st Judge Othniel - 40 yrs
2573 2nd Judge Ehud - 80 yrs
2651 3rd Judge Shamger
2654 4th Judge Deborah (with Barak) - 40 yrs
2694 5th Judge Gideon - 40 yrs
2734 6th Judge Abimelech - 3 yrs
2737 7th Judge Tola - 23 yrs
2758 8th Judge Jair - 22 yrs
2779 9th Judge Jeptheth - 6 yrs
2781 2nd yr of Jepthath and 300 yr mark
2785 10th Judge Ibzan - 7yrs
2792 11th Judge Elon - 10 yrs
2802 12th Judge Abdon - 8 yrs
2810 13th Judge Samson - 20 yrs
2830 14th Judge Eli the high Priest - 40 yrs
2871 15th Judge Samuel the Prophet - 13 years*
2882 King Saul*
2892 King David
2924 King Solomon
2928 Solomon lays the foundation of the Temple
2935 Solomon dedicates the Temple
2964 Rehoboam - 17 yrs
2969 Shishak of Egypt invades
2981 Abijam - 3 yrs
2983 Asa - 41 yrs
2999 Zerah the Nubian attacked
3019 Baasha attacked Judah
3024 Jehoshaphat - 25 yrs
3047 Jehoram II - 8yrs
3055 Ahaziah II - 1 yr

Ancient Post-Flood History

3056   Athaliah - 7 yrs
3061   Joash - 23 yrs
3084   Joash renovated the Temple
3100   Amaziah
3115   Uzziah
3167   Jotham
3183   Ahaz
3199   Hezekiah
3228   Manasseh
3283   Amon
3285   Josiah
3302   Josiah renovated the Temple
3316   Jehoahaz II - 3 months
3316   Jehoiakim - 11 yrs
3327   Jehoiachin - 3mths (18 yrs old)
3327   Zedekiah
3336   Jerusalem besieged
3338   First Temple destroyed
3338   End of the 850 years in Israel

*Samuel and Saul co-ruled

Appendix B
Timeline of Gentile Kings
From the Jasher Scroll

Year	Event
1557	Noah Begat Ham
1656	Noah's Flood
????	Ham begat Mitzraim. Mitzraim founded Egypt
????	Mitzraim begat Anom (Anom became the god, Amon-Ra) - Jasher 7:11
????	Anom begat Oswiris (Oswiris became the god, Osiris) - Jasher 14:2
????	Rikayn usurped throne and became first Pharaoh - Jasher 14
2018	Abraham given The Promise (the 430 years begins; Gal. 3:16,17)
2023	Abraham went to Egypt and saw Rikayon and Oswiris – Jasher 14,15
2039	War between Chittim and Tubal (Rape of the Sabines) began
2047	Sabine war ended
	Rikayon begat ... Gap of 209-212 years
2216	Joseph sold into Egypt - Jasher 59
2228	Joseph interpreted Pharaoh's dream - Jasher 59
2238	Jacob (130) went to Egypt
2255	Jacob died, Zepho captured - Jasher 56-57
2270	Magron (Son of Joseph's Pharaoh) became Pharaoh - Jasher 58
2288	Sons of Jacob fought with the sons of Esau
2309	Joseph died.
2310	Magron died. Zepho fled from Egypt to Angeas of Africa
????	Angeas of Africa wared with Turnus of Bibentu - Jasher 60 - Unknown Pharaoh rules from 2310 to 2340, or thirty years
2313	Zepho fled from Angeas of Africa to Chittim
????	Angeas built aqueducts for water
????	Zepho repeled Angeas from Chittim
2317	Zepho united all of Italy and became the first Roman King. - Jasher 62:1
2329	Africa attacked Chittim - Jasher 62:25
2340	Zepho destroyed African invasion fleet - Jasher 63

Ancient Post-Flood History

Year Event

????	Angeas and Lucas attacked Chittim - Edom refused to help Chittim - Zepho prayed
????	Chittim (Zepho) and Edom attacked Egypt and lost
2353	Melol became Pharaoh - Jasher 63:4,9
2367	Janeas became king of Rome
2368	Moses born
2386	Moses killed the Egyptian and fled to the land of Cush - Jasher 71
2395	King Kikianus of Cush died and Moses is made king of Cush.- Jasher 73
2411	Angeas king of Africa died, Azdrubal his son took his throne - Jahser 74
2417	Janeas, king of Rome, died and Latinus became king of Rome - Jasher 74
2421	Latinus of Rome attacked Azdrubal of Africa. Azdrubal died and his brother Anibal became king of Africa
2421	Anibal wared with Rome - Jasher 74
2437	Melol fell sick for ten years - Jasher 77:3
2444	Adikam (son of Melol) became Pharaoh - Jasher 77:1,3
2448	Adikam did not return to Egypt Jasher 81:40,41
2448	The Exodus
2448	God gave the Ten Commandments (the 430 years ended; Gal 3:16,17)
2462	King Latinus of Rome died - Jasher 74
2463	Abianus became king of Rome
2488	Israel entered Canaan under Joshua.
2494	Abianus captured Edom
2501	Abianus died and Latinus II became king of Rome - Jasher 90:28,29
2505	Rule of the Judges began in Israel
2551	Latinus II died

Other Books By Ken Johnson, Th.D.

Ancient Post-Flood History

Ancient Seder Olam
A Christian Translation of the 2000-year-old Scroll

This 2000-year-old scroll reveals the chronology from Creation through Cyrus' decree that freed the Jews in 536 BC. The *Ancient Seder Olam* uses biblical prophecy to prove its calculations of the timeline. We have used this technique to continue the timeline all the way to the reestablishment of the nation of Israel in AD 1948.

Using the Bible and rabbinical tradition, this book shows that the ancient Jews awaited King Messiah to fulfill the prophecy spoken of in Daniel, Chapter 9. The Seder answers many questions about the chronology of the books of Kings and Chronicles. It talks about the coming of Elijah, King Messiah's reign, and the battle of Gog and Magog.

This scroll and the Jasher scroll are the two main sources used in Ken's first book, *Ancient Post-Flood History*.

Ancient Prophecies Revealed
500 Prophecies Listed In Order Of When They Were Fulfilled

This book details over 500 biblical prophecies in the order they were fulfilled; these include pre-flood times through the First Coming of Jesus and into the Middle Ages. The heart of this book is the fifty-three prophecies fulfilled between 1948 and 2008. The last fifteen prophecies between 2008 and the Tribulation are also given. All these are documented and interpreted from the Ancient Church Fathers.

The Ancient Church Fathers, including disciples of the twelve apostles, were firmly premillennial, pretribulational, and very pro-Israel.

Ancient Post-Flood History

Ancient Book of Jasher
Referenced in Joshua 10:13; 2 Samuel 1:18; 2 Timothy 3:8

There are thirteen ancient history books cited and recommended by the Bible. The Ancient Book of Jasher is the only one of the thirteen that still exists. It is referenced in Joshua 10:13; 2 Samuel 1:18; and 2 Timothy 3:8. This volume contains the entire ninety-one chapters plus a detailed analysis of the supposed discrepancies, cross-referenced historical accounts, and detailed charts for ease of use. As with any history book, there are typographical errors in the text but with three consecutive timelines running through the histories, it is very easy to arrive at the exact dates of recorded events. It is not surprising that this ancient document confirms the Scripture and the chronology given in the Hebrew version of the Old Testament, once and for all settling the chronology differences between the Hebrew Old Testament and the Greek Septuagint.

Third Corinthians
Ancient Gnostics and the End of the World

This little known, 2000-year-old Greek manuscript was used in the first two centuries to combat Gnostic cults. Whether or not it is an authentic copy of the original epistle written by the apostle Paul, it gives an incredible look into the cults that will arise in the Last Days. It contains a prophecy that the same heresies that pervaded the first century church would return before the Second Coming of the Messiah.

Ancient Post-Flood History

Ancient Paganism
The Sorcery of the Fallen Angels

Ancient Paganism explores the false religion of the ancient pre-Flood world and its spread into the Gentile nations after Noah's Flood. Quotes from the ancient church fathers, rabbis, and the Talmud detail the activities and beliefs
of both Canaanite and New Testament era sorcery. This book explores how, according to biblical prophecy, this same sorcery will return before the Second Coming of Jesus Christ to earth. These religious beliefs and practices will invade the end time church and become the basis for the religion of the Antichrist. Wicca, Druidism, Halloween, Yule, meditation, and occultic tools are discussed at length.

The Rapture

The Pretribulational Rapture of the Church Viewed From the Bible and the Ancient Church

This book presents the doctrine of the pretribulational Rapture of the church. Many prophecies are explored with Biblical passages and terms explained.

Evidence is presented that proves the first century church believed the End Times would begin with the return of Israel to her ancient homeland, followed by the Tribulation and the Second Coming. More than fifty prophecies have been fulfilled since Israel became a state.

Evidence is also given that several ancient rabbis and at least four ancient church fathers taught a pretribulational Rapture. This book also gives many of the answers to the arguments midtribulationists and posttribulationists use. It is our hope this book will be an indispensable guide for debating the doctrine of the Rapture.

Ancient Epistle of Barnabas
His Life and Teaching

The Epistle of Barnabas is often quoted by the ancient church fathers. Although not considered inspired Scripture, it was used to combat legalism in the first two centuries AD. Besides explaining why the Laws of Moses are not binding on Christians, the Epistle explains how many of the Old Testament rituals teach typological prophecy. Subjects explored are: Yom Kippur, the Red Heifer ritual, animal sacrifices, circumcision, the Sabbath, Daniel's visions and the end-time ten nation empire, and the Temple.

The underlying theme is the Three-Fold Witness. Barnabas teaches that mature Christians must be able to lead people to the Lord, testify to others about Bible prophecy fulfilled in their lifetimes, and teach creation history and creation science to guard the faith against the false doctrine of evolution. This is one more ancient church document that proves the first century church was premillennial and constantly looking for the Rapture and other prophecies to be fulfilled.

The Ancient Church Fathers
What the Disciples of the Apostles Taught

This book reveals who the disciples of the twelve apostles were and what they taught, from their own writings. It documents the same doctrine was faithfully transmitted to their descendants in the first few centuries and where, when, and by whom, the doctrines began to change. The ancient church fathers make it very easy to know for sure what the complete teachings of Jesus and the twelve apostles were.

You will learn, from their own writings, that the first century disciples taught on the various doctrines that divide our church today. You will learn what was discussed at the seven general councils and why. You will learn who were the cults and cult leaders that began to change doctrine and spread their heresy and how that became to be the standard teaching in the medieval church. A partial list of doctrines discussed in this book are:

Abortion	Free will	Purgatory
Animals sacrifices	Gnostic cults	Psychology
Antichrist	Homosexuality	Reincarnation
Arminianism	Idolatry	Replacement theology
Bible or tradition	Islam	Roman Catholicism
Calvinism	Israel's return	The Sabbath
Circumcision	Jewish food laws	Salvation
Deity of Jesus Christ	Mary's virginity	Schism of Nepos
Demons	Mary's assumption	Sin / Salvation
Euthanasia	Meditation	The soul
Evolution	The Nicolaitans	Spiritual gifts
False gospels	Paganism	Transubstantiation
False prophets	Predestination	Yoga
Foreknowledge	premillennialism	Women in ministry

For more information visit us at:

Biblefacts.org

Bibliography

1. Cruse, C. F., *Eusebius' Ecclesiastical History*, Hendrickson Publishers, 1998.
2. Eerdmans Publishing, *Ante-Nicene Fathers*, Eerdmans Publishing, 1886.
3. Keating, Geoffrey, *The History of Ireland (BOOK I-II),* London, Irish Texts Society, 1902.
4. Johnson, Ken, *Ancient Seder Olam*, Createspace, 2006.
5. Johnson, Ken, *Ancient Book of Jasher*, Createspace, 2008
6. R. H. Charles, *The Book of Jubilees*, FQ Classics, 2007
7. Hodges, Richmond, *Cory's Ancient Fragments*, London, Reeves and Turner, 1876.
8. Whiston, William, *The Works of Flavius Josephus*, London, Miller & Sowerby, 1987. Includes Antiquities of the Jews.
9. Pezron, Paul, *The Antiquities of Nations*, Mr. D. Jones, translator (London: R. Janeway, publisher, 1706.
10. Karlgren, Bernhard, *Legends and Cults in Ancient China*, Reprint. Philadelphia, PA: Porcupine Press, Incorporated, 1985.
11. Long, James, *The Riddle of the Exodus*, Lightcatcher Books, 2002.
12. Louis Ginzberg, *The Legends of the Jews*, Johns Hopkins University Press, 1948.
13. Robert W. Thomson, *Rewriting Caucasian History*, Clarendon Press, 1996
14. Kang, C H, *The Discovery of Genesis*, Concordia Publishing House, 1979

Notes:

Notes:

Notes:

18492619R00101

Made in the USA
Lexington, KY
09 November 2012